MERCEDES-BENZ SALOONS

The Classic Models of the 1960s and 1970s

Other titles in the Crowood AutoClassic Series

MERCEDES-BENZ SALOONS

The Classic Models of the 1960s and 1970s

Laurence Meredith

The Crowood Press

First published in 2003 by
The Crowood Press Ltd
Ramsbury, Marlborough
Wiltshire SN8 2HR

www.crowood.com

British Library Cataloguing-in-Publication Data
A catalogue record for this book is available from the British Library.

ISBN 1 86126 518 2

Acknowledgements

The author is grateful to: Martin Cushway, Ron Cushway, Nigel Phillips, Huw Meredith, Gerry Doverman, Mark Cole and DaimlerChrysler.

Designed and typeset by
Focus Publishing
11a St Botolph's Road
Sevenoaks
Kent TN13 1AP

Contents

By the 1960s Daimler-Benz had begun developing cars for a new era in which passenger safety would be of paramount importance. Brutal and comprehensive crash testing would result in the world's safest cars being built in Stuttgart.

The Ponton series of the 1950s served their purpose well, and brought profits for Daimler-Benz at a time when arch-rival BMW was producing similar cars that nearly brought the Munich company to the brink of financial disaster.

Introduction

In 2001, DaimlerChrysler celebrated the centenary of the Mercedes name. In Britain, this milestone was marked by a feast of historically important Mercs – past and present – appearing at the Goodwood Festival of Speed. For Mercedes fans this was a grand occasion that provided an opportunity to reflect on the Stuttgart company's great achievements, not least of which was the invention of the motor car itself, of course.

At about the same time as the Festival of Speed, a new Mercedes-Benz dealership was publicly opened in Germany's 'new' capital city, Berlin. A vast and aesthetically interesting steel and glass structure, it boasts 150,000 square feet of display space on four floors. The building includes a restaurant, with a 750-year-old olive tree, a water garden with palm trees, two climbing walls to provide training facilities for the German Alpine Club, and a 400-square-foot video screen for the broadcasting of footage from the Grand Prix circus. The new Berlin dealership building attracts thousands of visitors, most of whom have no intention of buying a new or second-hand Mercedes. The structure, with its many facilities, is a remarkable achievement of modern architecture and a superb reflection of DaimlerChrysler's commitment to remaining at the forefront of automotive retailing in the twenty-first century.

Staying ahead of the game has been a recurring theme in the long history of this great company, and one reason for its continuing success in global markets. Although several models in the range over the years have presented a rather conservative image, the people charged with responsibility for the future of this vast concern are among the most radical thinkers in the industry. It would be easy for them to sit back, rest on Mercedes' laurels, and see the whole lot slide into the bin. Instead, the people at Mercedes are acutely aware of their responsibilities, of the massive economic shockwaves being created by 'globalization', and of the intense competition presented by rivals.

The threat from BMW in Munich is exceptionally strong and ever-present, and the rivalry between the two car giants has resulted in increasingly interesting marketing tactics – as well as splendid and innovative motor cars. More recently, the efforts of Dr Ferdinand Piëch, as head of Audi, have thrown a spanner in the works for both BMW and Mercedes.

This is the point at which the big German players find themselves today. The journey up to this point began, more or less, at the beginning of the 1960s. The start of this decade of massive change saw the introduction of a new and modern range of Mercedes cars, incorporating many innovations, largely pioneered by Bela Barenyi. For journalists and for the car-buying public, it was an exciting period. It also marked the beginning of BMW's recovery from the brink of financial oblivion.

The pioneering work by Barenyi and his team – mostly related to improvements in safety – included the adoption of bodyshells with side-impact beams in the doors, a rigid pas-

By the beginning of the 1970s the luxurious S-Class saloons had set new standards in all areas of car design, reflecting an era of affluence.

senger safety cell, with deformable front and rear 'crumple' zones, and research into airbags. Today, some manufacturers still proclaim the advantages of airbags in their advertising campaigns, but Mercedes began work in this area as long ago as 1966. After investing £9 million in research and development, Mercedes first offered airbags as extra-cost options on the S Class saloon from 1981, some years before others would even think about them. By 1992, more than one million Mercs equipped with airbags had found satisfied customers.

During the 1960s, the Mercedes saloons were brought into the modern era, although the long-held tenets of durability, quality, safety and performance remained intact. Body

styling, however, marked something of a radical departure from traditional Mercedes values. As the company had gained a valuable foot in its most important export market, the USA, during the 1950s, it was almost inevitable that some design features would pander to American taste. The changes failed to find universal favour, however; many thousands of customers bought German cars specifically for their distinctly European styling. A mid-Atlantic 'halfway-house' was, with the wisdom of hindsight, something of a mistake, but Mercedes-Benz continued to prosper all the same.

While the saloons of this classic period were respected as the benchmark by which all others of their ilk would be measured, Daimler-Benz's board chose to sell their products on merit. After a terrible and fatal accident at Le Mans in 1955, involving Pierre Levegh's Mercedes-Benz 300SLR sports car, there were no factory sporting programmes to act as a sales tool in the showrooms, Daimler-Benz would return to high-profile motor racing – with sports cars in the 1980s, and Grand Prix in the 1990s – but throughout the 1960s and 70s, involvement in top-flight competition was minimal. BMW took full advantage of the Stuttgart company's absence from the circuits during this period, and the results are only too plain to appreciate today.

Although so many of the Mercedes saloons from the 60s and 70s have been accorded classic status, they were not without their critics. Because of purchase tax, their cost in Britain (as with other foreign cars) was artificially high, which naturally raised eyebrows in certain sectors of the motoring media. Beyond this there was a certain amount of vitriol aimed at Mercedes' over-large steering wheels, minimal instrumentation and 'soft' suspension, but these criticisms were seen as mere nitpicking by the company's loyal clientele.

The star emblem became famous throughout the globe as a symbol of social prestige, and of solid, dependable engineering, and the cars were as popular among heads of state as they were among taxi drivers. Supremely comfortable and pleasant to drive, a Merc is certainly different from any other car. BMWs may generally have the sporting edge, but there is little doubting the unique solidity, confidence and calming effect of a Mercedes.

During the 1960s and 70s, developments in the motor industry were proceeding at a pace, with Porsche and Daimler-Benz pioneering the most important innovations. In many respects the Mercedes saloons, particularly of the 1970s, were every bit as advanced and modern as the cars emerging from Sindelfingen today. There is little doubt that they remain as greats among the classics. The S-Class saloons in particular hold a special place in the hearts of nostalgic Merc devotees. Large, bold, fast, supremely able and undeniably menacing, these superior machines encompassed the laudable idea of automotive elitism – they were predators without rival.

This concept has contributed to a certain polarization of views about the cars from Daimler-Benz. Many love them; others loathe them. The latter may also be influenced by the

Despite its global reputation as a luxury-car maker, Daimler-Benz has for many years catered for the 'lower' end of the market with solid, reliable cars built to the same standard as the machines in the upper echelons.

The cars of the 1970s were so advanced and well made that original, or restored, examples feel good to drive even by today's high standards.

regrettable anti-German sentiment that exists in some sections of British society. Yet no one can deny the superiority of the engineering from the German companies of Mercedes, BMW, Porsche and Volkswagen, particularly in comparison with British cars of the post-war period, many of which served only as a bad example to the rest of the automotive industry.

Many of the Mercs from this particular period have survived, and continue to prosper in the hands of enthusiasts on both sides of the Atlantic. Mercedes owners are extremely well catered for; virtually all parts are readily available, and the thriving restoration industry is capable of keeping these old cars going for as long as their owners are prepared to pay for them.

The launch of a new Mercedes–Benz is an exciting event, providing an opportunity to study and enjoy the work of talented designers and engineers, but looking to the company's past achievements is equally satisfying. Surely most historians who study the motor industry would prefer to dwell on a classic Mercedes, rather than on some anodyne modern design?

Mercedes: A Brief History

The first wheeled vehicle powered by an internal combustion engine was designed by Karl Benz and publicly debuted in 1886. With help from Paul Daimler and Wilhelm Maybach, the concept of the motor car was quickly developed; by 1903, the 60HP Mercedes – the name was adopted by dealer and enthusiast Emil Jellinek after his favourite daughter – had become a sophisticated and fast machine capable of carrying people reliably over vast distances.

The slightly later 90HP Mercedes was capable of a top speed of more than 90mph (145km/h), at a time when the vast majority of people living in western Europe travelled by bicycle, horse or Shanks's pony. Motor racing, which began in France, served to hasten the development during these important pioneering days, and by the outbreak of the Great War in 1914, some manufacturers had already discovered the advantages of, for example, overhead camshafts and multi-valve cylinders heads.

Along with the great car manufacturers of Britain, Italy and France, Mercedes built exciting machines for both road and track, the four nations competing fiercely for supremacy over each other. In 1926, rivals Daimler and Benz merged into one company – Daimler-Benz – and produced cars from this time under the Mercedes-Benz banner.

During the period that followed, Professor Porsche's engineering and design genius was to have a profound effect at Daimler-Benz, and the Stuttgart company producing acknowledged classics in the form of the mighty SS series sports cars. After Porsche went on to found his own company in 1930, much of Daimler-Benz's development work was carried out under the guidance of Rudi Uhlenhaut. This was an era in which German innovation came to the fore. Between 1934 and the outbreak of the Second World War, motor racing in particular entered one of its golden periods, with the Porsche-designed Auto-Union Grand Prix machines slugging it out with equally sophisticated hardware from Daimler-Benz.

After the war, Daimler-Benz, along with many other German industrial concerns, struggled to recover. The company's factories were attacked during 1944 by Allied bombing raids, and lay in ruin. However, by 1947, production of saloon cars had resumed and, as demand began to rise, profits were reinvested in new plant, machinery and products. Exports started to earn the company healthy returns by the early 1950s, and in 1952 a brace of Mercedes-Benz 300SL coupés placed first and second in the Le Mans 24 Hours. The publicity that ensued from this victory brought Daimler-Benz under the international spotlight once again. Throughout 1954 and 1955, the company's racing cars were hugely successful in both Grand Prix and international sports-car racing.

Tragedy was to strike at Le Mans in 1955, when Pierre Levegh's 300SLR was launched into the crowd from the rear of Lance Macklin's Healey. This terrible accident, motor racing's worst ever, killed Levegh and more than 80 spectators. As a result, Daimler-Benz withdrew from international motor sport until the 1980s when it once again entered the world of top-level sports-car racing.

From 1955 onwards, Daimler-Benz concentrated its efforts on high-quality saloons, and sports/GT cars for road use. Many were expensive and glamorous, and they were always beautifully made. As exports began to spiral inexorably upwards, the company's reputation for quality and excellence grew in direct proportion. Competition, particularly from BMW and Jaguar from 1968, saw Daimler-Benz step up into top gear to stay ahead; new models were launched and always genuinely improved.

Oil crises, stringent rules and regulations governing car safety and exhaust emissions, marketing demands and competition from other manufacturers have all conspired to challenge the clever people working in Stuttgart. Over many years, healthy sales figures have demonstrated that the company that invented the motor car remains ahead today.

Outright victory at Le Mans, and elsewhere, in 1989, the launch of a host of exciting sports cars and saloons in the 1990s, and the design of a championship-winning engine for the Formula One McLaren team, also in the 1990s, are all part and parcel of the company's programme of staying on top today.

In the late 1990s, Daimler-Benz merged with US giant Chrysler, to form DaimlerChrysler. With the spiralling costs of research and development, the stressful demands of product liability laws, especially in the USA, and the many other complex demands of the global market, this mutually convenient arrangement was intended to ensure the continued success and competitiveness of both companies during the twenty-first century.

For more than a century the Mercedes name has been synonymous with quality, innovation, prestige and design integrity. At the beginning of the new millennium, the company's reputation shows no sign of decline, its fortunes illustrating the constant need for progress in a sea of relentless automotive change.

1 A Tale of Fins from Germany

Moving into the 1960s

By any normal mortal standards it must have been difficult for Stuttgart's top talent to move from the 1950s into the 1960s. The company's 300SL sports coupés had finished first and second at Le Mans in 1952, Stirling Moss and Denis Jenkinson had trounced the opposition in the 1955 Mille Miglia with the 300SLR, and Fangio had secured his third Grand Prix Championship with the W196 in the same year.

On a more mundane note, the production cars were selling well at all levels, and in increasing numbers. The 300SL 'Gullwing' was an exception, of course, but this extraordinary machine – the world's first true supercar – was created as a technical flagship. For this reason, its lack of commercial success did not matter a jot.

After Pierre Levegh's accident in the Mercedes at Le Mans in 1955, which resulted in the death of 84 people, the company's sports racing programme ended. The Grand Prix cars competed in just two more races during 1955 – Silverstone and Monza – and that was that. The competition department was closed, a decision heavily influenced by the Le Mans tragedy, but the cost was officially cited as the reason for the cessation of racing activities. Money that would otherwise be directed towards motor racing would be invested in new road cars and important development work.

Perceived as dependable, well made, durable and luxurious, and perhaps even

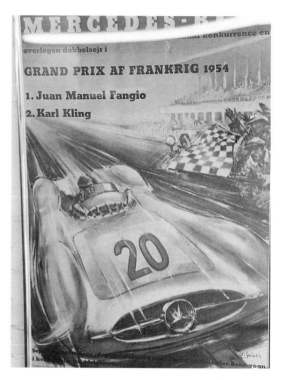

Daimler-Benz's supremacy in international motor sport between its Le Mans victory 1952 and the end of the 1955 season at Monza was almost unrivalled. A fatal accident at the 1955 Le Mans, however, would result in Mercedes' absence from top-level motor sport until the 1980s.

slightly stolid and conservative, the Mercs of the 1950s had succeeded in a market in which BMW had clearly failed. While the Munich company hung on by the skin of its teeth by producing economical microcars, Daimler-Benz, along with Porsche, were able to invest in new projects (although Porsche differed from Mercedes in that it remained committed to a comprehensive competition programme).

From an early stage, however, it became apparent to all European manufacturers that, whether they supported showroom sales with competition activity or not, it was imperative to break into the lucrative North American market. Neither the USA nor Canada had had its infrastructure damaged by the Second World War, and citizens in both countries had a significant amount of money to spend.

Throughout the 1950s, Mercedes sold relatively few passenger saloons in either Cana-

Stolid, dependable and durable, the 1950s Ponton range of 4- and 6-cylinder cars was a typically conservative product of post-war Germany – no-nonsense, no frills and few thrills, but highly capable.

da or the USA. Detroit seemed to be keeping the North American market happy, with a variety of cars, ranging from the ugly to the outrageous. It was an era of wild American excess and questionable taste; sadly, several European manufacturers, including Daimler-Benz, chose to pander to American demands, for wholly mercenary reasons. The sensuous and elegant body curves of the 1950s suddenly became unfashionable (except in the notable case of Porsche's increasingly important Volkswagen Beetle), and the 'clean-shaven', 'crisply ironed' look came into vogue.

From the sporting 300SL Roadster of the late 1950s to the sober 230SL of 1963, Daimler-Benz had completely changed direction. It was a move embodied in the change from the Ponton saloons of the 1950s to the Fintails of the following decade.

Ponton styling was typically European and characteristic of the 1950s, but Detroit's influence would lead to radical change by the start of the 1960s, as Mercedes sought to exploit the potentially lucrative US market.

Battered, Crumpled and Polished

Work on the new breed of Fintail saloons began in the mid-1950s under the stewardship of Dr Fritz Nallinger, a chap known for his precise manner. His team of dedicated experts were all committed to the common goal of adhering to the highest attainable engineering standards. Nothing less would have been acceptable from Daimler-Benz; indeed, it never has been.

Testing of the khaki-coloured prototypes began in the miserably cold weather of January 1958. In time-honoured fashion, the hand-built test mules were heavily disguised, but, by thrashing across Europe for a couple of million miles in convoy with contemporary Mercedes saloons, the company was fooling no one.

Other development work was conducted in complete secrecy. Nallinger had drawn up a set of dimensions around which the new saloon would be built, and the rest was up to the engineers. The great Rudi Uhlenhaut was charged with responsibility for chassis development, Karl Wilfert with bodywork, and Josef Müller with engine work.

Publicly unveiled at the 1959 Frankfurt Show, three new 6-cylinder models (W111) were offered as a replacement for the outgoing Ponton equivalents. Officially the 220b, 220Sb and 220SEb, but badged without the 'b' suffix, the new cars clearly established the foundations for further development as the 1960s unfolded.

Above *The new range of Fintails (*Heckflosse *in German) emerged in 1959 under the leadership of Fritz Nallinger, with a styling package designed to appeal to both European and American taste.*

Research on the new range started in the mid-1950s; extensive crash testing and development resulted in the first passenger cars with a central 'safety cell'. Other manufacturers would eventually follow suit.

Instantly dubbed 'Fintails', or *Heckflosse* in German, after their distinctive American-style rear wings, the cars were exceptionally well received by journalists. Interestingly, the *Autocar* November 1959 road test, possibly in an attempt to be diplomatic, failed to deliver an opinion on the new styling. However, it was wholly unequivocal in its praise for the 220SE's roadability and dynamics. *Autocar*'s reporter made it clear that the car was improved in every way over the outgoing model:

> The 220SE has outstanding road manners, undoubtedly allied to the firm's long experience in racing. In addition, it permits the achievement of high and sustained cruising speeds with very good economy. The interior is planned to carry five people and their luggage over long distances, in a manner matched by very few other cars, irrespective of their country of origin. Except for the frontal aspect, its styling is thoroughly in keeping with modern thought and, in a phrase, it seems to have been planned by men who are aware of the niceties and refinements necessary for those who will appreciate good motoring.

The report in *The Motor*, similarly, concentrated on the car's technical merits: 'Second only to performance, the most striking thing about the 220SE is its controllability.'

Interestingly, while contemporary reports about Ferraris and Maseratis led with prosaic eulogy about Italian styling, Bill Boddy, editor of the once-revered *Motor Sport*, wrote simply that Mercs were the best cars in the world.

220SEb (W111) 1959–65 saloon, 1961–65 coupé and convertible	
Body style	Four-door saloon, two-door coupé and convertible
Engine	
Cylinders	6
Bore × stroke	80mm × 72.8mm
Capacity	2195cc
Timing	Single-overhead camshaft
Compression ratio	8.7:1
Fuel system	Bosch mechanical fuel injection
Max power	120bhp at 4,800rpm
Max torque	140lb ft at 3,900rpm
Transmission	
Gearbox	Four-speed manual or optional automatic from August 1961
Suspension and steering	
Front	Independent by wishbones, coil springs and anti-roll bar
Rear	Swing-axles, coil springs and telescopic dampers
Steering	Daimler Benz recirculating ball
Wheels	Pressed-steel 5.5J×13
Brakes	Servo-assisted drums, front discs on coupé and convertible
Dimensions	
Track	(front) 58.3in (1457.5mm) (rear) 58.3in (1457.5mm)
Overall length	192.1in (4802.5mm)
Overall width	72.7in (1817.5mm)
Overall height	57in (1425mm)

Brains in a Body

Despite having a wheelbase 3in (75mm) shorter than the Ponton model, the overall length of the Fintail's body was increased by 5in (125mm) and the width by 3in (75mm). These changes inevitably led to greater space for passengers and luggage, and improved primary safety, but incurred a weight penalty of around 50lb (23kg).

Of unitary construction – the first evidence that Mercedes had arrived in the modern world in this respect – the body was particularly special in that it comprised a central passenger safety cell, with 'crumple' zones fore and aft. Sometimes referred to as 'the father of passive safety', Bela Barenyi had invented this idea in the early 1950s; there is hardly a designer that has not been forced to copy it.

The Fintail was a large four-door saloon, its dimensions clearly based on those of its contemporaries from Detroit. The styling drew inspiration from Italy and the USA. At the front there was the inevitable chromed radiator grille – tall and imposing, with the three-pointed star standing out proudly at the top. Tough, double-bladed bumpers added to the car's weighty appearance, but the novel headlamps (*Lichtenheiten*), first introduced on the

17

Above *Boot space was large by European standards, and one reason why these big saloons became popular with taxi drivers and other commercial operators.*

Left *A strong and attractive styling feature, the* Lichtenheiten, *or 'stacked' headlamp lenses as they are sometimes known, were first seen on the 300SL Roadster in 1957.*

Below *Wheels were of vented pressed steel with a five-stud fitting. Alloys would become available in 1969, and then only as extra-cost options.*

300SL Roadster in 1957, made the Merc stand out from the herd.

Early James Bond films, starring Sean Connery, featured a number of Fintails, usually painted black, and always driven by 'baddies'. Their frontal appearance means that these cars will probably be for ever associated with sinister glamour.

In contrast with the cars of the previous era, the flanks on the Fintail were slab-sided, the aching tracts of sheet metal broken by a swage line that swept downwards towards the rear. The latter treatment complemented and contrasted with the fins atop the rear wings, which, with the wisdom of hindsight, was something of a mistake. Mercedes had its own, very strong identity without having to adapt to prevailing American taste, but it would be a few years before these appendages were abandoned.

Extensive external brightwork reflected the growing affluence in Europe. By the 1980s, embellishment with chromium plating would be considered unnecessary in some quarters, and vulgar in others.

Above *An official publicity shot from Daimler-Benz of an early 6-cylinder Fintail, showing the whitewall tyres, which were not as popular in Europe as they were in the USA.*

Below *The Fintail's dashboard was heavily padded as a concession to passenger safety. The 'no-nonsense' steering wheel was overly large, but comfortable enough in use.*

The Fintail's rump was finished with heavy, double-bladed bumpers, similar to the ones at the front, and broad 'strip' lights, which also added to the Germanic-cum-American appearance. The window glass area was commendably large for the period – a modern safety factor – but not as large as on the mid-range BMW saloons that debuted just three years later, in 1962. Despite the presence of the vertically positioned spare wheel, the boot space was impressively large, too.

This late 1950s shot is typical of contemporary publicity material from German manufacturers, which sought to portray a glamorous lifestyle. Only the well-heeled could afford to fly, and to buy a Mercedes-Benz.

Keen motor-sport fan Martin Cushway has converted his 220SE for historic rallying, with additional instruments and a Halda Twinmaster.

Below *The spacious interior could comfortably seat five, with generous legroom, but the firmly upholstered seats offered little in the way of lateral support.*

By contrast with the front seats in the standard car, Martin Cushway has fitted modern bucket-style seats to his rally car, with improved body support for hard cornering.in the way of lateral support.

At 13in, the pressed-steel wheels were relatively small in diameter (in a trend that would be largely reversed in the 1990s), and closed, with 'all-enveloping' hubcaps. It is tempting to conclude that alloy wheels were not used on these expensive cars simply because they had not been sufficiently developed, but this would be to ignore Bugatti's Type 35, 41, 46 and 49; all of these were fitted with alloys between the late 1920s and mid-1930s.

Like all cars in its class, the big Merc was decorated with brightwork. Although chromi-um plating is eschewed in the modern world, in those days fashion dictated that it would not have been a proper luxury car without such embellishment.

Overall, the body styling was not especially remarkable, but it was entirely practical. Some struggled to warm to the car on aesthetic grounds, but it certainly compared favourably with models such as the Ford Classic, or its American contemporary, the Edsel.

Padded Cell

With its super-safe rigid structure, the new car also had an interior that broke new ground. With the aim of reducing the possibility of injury as a result of a high-speed collision, it incorporated flexible switchgear, soft padding where there would normally have been painted metal, a padded central boss to the steering wheel and a rear-view mirror designed to snap from its mounting in the event of impact.

Some 10 years after Daimler-Benz introduced these safety-related features, American legislation made them compulsory; once again, the politicians had lagged way behind the technocrats.

In contrast with modern parallel windscreen wipers, the Fintails had a revised version of the old-fashioned 'clap-hands' variety, which cleared a greater part of the screen. Along with Citroën, Daimler-Benz would carry this idea further forward in future years by adopting a single wiper.

By European standard the Fintail's interior was especially voluminous and comfortable. However, *The Motor* was moved to comment that 'the difficult aim of fitting all human shapes is not quite achieved, for a long unbroken journey found one driver in need of more padding behind the small of his back'. On the other hand, the reporters acknowledged that, 'for rear-seat passengers … there is ample space in all dimensions and the large window area

Largely pandering to American taste, the styling of the speedometer came in for almost universal condemnation, and the 'umbrella-type' handbrake lever under the dashboard was also out of kilter with European tradition.

makes it possible for everybody to see out without being perched too high for comfort'.

Cloth-, Tex- (vinyl), or leather-covered (at extra cost), the seats were expansive, well crafted and characteristically durable. By comparison with similar versions from Jaguar and Rolls-Royce, the leather seats were not especially pretty, but they served their purpose well enough. Even less appealing was the 'wooden' dashboard trim – actually made of plastic – although, with its ability to resist splintering in an accident, it certainly contributed to the car's impressive list of safety features.

Particularly praiseworthy was the new inte-rior ventilation system, which distributed air from a collection 'box' in front of the wind-screen base, and distributed it, via a variable-speed blower, throughout the cabin.

For added comfort, all four doors were fit-ted with armrests, and an additional thickly bolstered armrest was provided for the centre of the rear seats.

For Weddings and the Odd Funeral

Daimler-Benz's products needed to compete head-on with their contemporaries, particu-larly from Cadillac. The major instruments and controls of the Fintail were distinctly Ameri-can in style – an 'umbrella'-style handbrake below the dashboard, a column-mounted gearstick (with an optional floor-mounted lever), and the infamous 'ribbon' speedometer

The interior door panelling and fittings were made to such a high standard that many examples survive in original condition.

– and were the subject of much criticism from European customers and journalists.

There was almost universal condemnation of the speedometer. The report in *The Motor* read as follows:

Rather surprisingly, the instrument cluster has succumbed to stylists' treatment, especially the speedometer, which is a wide vertical 'thermometer' strip with an angled top giving very vague readings. Notwithstanding a gimmick that

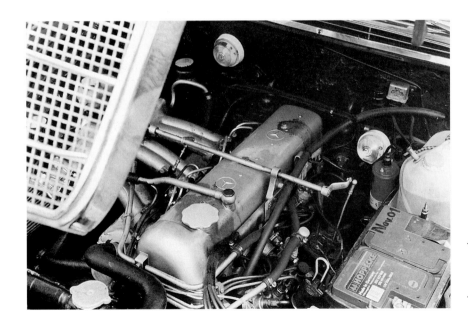

The first Fintails were all fitted with the same 2195cc 6-cylinder engine, but in different states of tune. The most powerful fuel-injected unit (shown here) developed 120bhp.

changes the colour of the strip from yellow to red when the speed exceeds 30mph [50km/h], the speedometer would be more helpful with a horizontal scale or an arc. It is in fact equivalent to a complete circular dial less than 1.5in [4cm] in diameter, or a semi-circular one 3in [7.5cm] across – for a range of 110mph [175km/h].

This style of speedometer was also used in a number of British cars, usually representing change for the sake of change, without actually improving upon traditional instrumentation.

At least the speedometer, distance recorder, fuel, water and oil pressure gauges were entirely 'on display'. The steering wheel saw to that. In Mercedes' traditional manner, it was perfectly light and positive in use, but of truck-like proportions.

Despite the inevitable criticism, few noticed these temporary aberrations when the car's primary purpose was properly exercised. There

was nothing garish to distract the driver, and nothing to detract from the sheer pleasure of cruising at high speed in near silence.

Writing in the English magazine *Country Life*, John Eason-Gibson commented as follows:

> As with all good cars, the 220SE was at its best on the open road, and it gave the impression that it would be untiring to drive over really long distances… Owing to the subdued instrument lighting, the lack of confusing reflections on the windscreen and the good headlamps driving after dark was very pleasant.

In the ultimate analysis, it mattered for very little that not everyone agreed about the interior's 'finer' points. Like so many Mercs through the years, the Fintail's bits and pieces were all beautifully made, felt completely solid and dependable, and looked virtually as new after many miles of hard use. There were no rattles and squeaks, even when the cars were driven over

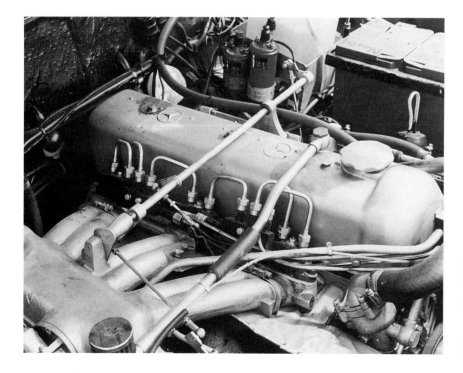

Mercedes was the first to introduce fuel-injection on a production petrol-engined car with the Gullwing in 1954. Volkswagen and Triumph would follow suit, but not until 1967.

Beautiful pieces of mechanical engineering in themselves, Bosch fuel pumps (this is the 6-plunger type) are generally very reliable, but have a tendency to dry out, leading to cracked seals after prolonged periods of disuse.

rough terrain, and even the Tex upholstery demonstrated its worth by outlasting virtually all other upholstery covers. It may have lacked the sporting finesse of a Mk2 Jaguar, the hand-crafted ambience of a Rolls-Royce, or the brashness of the chromium-encrusted models that were being knocked out in increasing numbers in Detroit, but this Merc's interior was still something a little bit special.

Power Bulge in the Front

All three of the original 6-cylinder Fintails were fitted with the same 7-bearing, overhead-camshaft 2195cc engine, but in different states of tune. At entry level the 220 gave 95bhp on twin carburettors, while the 220S, with a brace of twin-choke carburettors, developed 110bhp, and the fuel-injected 220SE delivered a maximum of 120bhp.

Contemporary journalists wrote of brisk acceleration, despite the increase in weight over the outgoing Pontons, and quickly discovered that each model was capable OF high-speed cruising without apparent effort. Top speeds varied from 100mph (160km/h) for the 'base' car, through 104mph (166km/h) for the 220S, to 110mph (177km/h) for the 220SE.

Until the advent of BMW's 'sixes' in 1968, Daimler-Benz's 6-cylinder power units were arguably among the most refined production units to be found anywhere, and received universal praise. *The Motor* described the unit as 'exceptionally smooth, even at tickover... and mechanically audible only at idling speed and above 5,000rpm in the gears, when it develops a slight hardness of tone which penetrates the very effective sound insulation'.

Interestingly, the same road testers discovered that the 220S was capable of matching the performance of the Bosch fuel-injected car, in both the mid- and top-speed range, and also had the added bonus of superior fuel consumption.

Although not in its infancy at this time, fuel injection had not been developed to the level of today's perfection. Daimler-Benz had manufactured the world's first production car with direct fuel injection in 1954 – the 300SL Gull-wing coupé. Transferring a similar system to the less exotic models was, of course, just a matter of time, and it undoubtedly had its advantages over carburettors.

Developed in conjunction with Bosch, the system delivered fuel through a fixed-calibration jet for each cylinder from a dual-plunger pump operated at engine speed. Timing of the fuel, as delivered to each cylinder, was varied according to valve opening, throttle setting and temperature. Both cold and hot starting were inherently efficient, although the carburettor models proved slightly better at starting from cold than the fuel-injected SE.

Autocar's early testers made the following comment on the 220SE:

> By far the most attractive feature of fuel injection is the flexibility it provides. For one part of the test journey there were five passengers; the luggage compartment was packed with their possessions and with road-test gear. So laden, the car could be slowed down to a trickle of no more than 8 to 10mph [13–16km/h] in top gear, and, when the throttle was slammed full open, it gained speed on quite an appreciable up gradient without a trace of hesitation or pinking from the engine.

At a maximum of 6,000rpm, *Motor*'s testers revealed the 'presence of a hard-working engine' that could be 'felt inside the car'. The magazine's 1959 report, however, admitted that 'at all other times the smoothness of performance matches a quite exceptional response to the rod–and–bellcrank accelerator control. Acceleration right up to 90mph [145km/h] is in what would ordinarily be regarded as the 3-litre class, and such features as oil/water heat exchanger are clearly designed in the expectation that the car will be driven very fast for long continuous periods.'

Britain's first production saloon with fuel injection – the Triumph 2500PI – was not launched until 1967, and its Lucas system was to prove troublesome for many owners on occasions. (One old joke claims that Lucas once made a prototype of a personal computer but, having failed to make it leak oil, did not bother with taking it into production!) However, despite the strides made by Bosch in the development of fuel injection for both Daimler-Benz and Volkswagen from 1968, British car buyers remained sceptical of its merits for many years – thanks to Lucas.

The Fintail's fuel consumption was typically 22mpg (13l/100km) in overall driving conditions, which prevailing wisdom considered to be acceptable for such a heavy car with a 6-cylinder engine. A contemporary 34bhp 1200 Volkswagen Beetle, by way of comparison, was capable of a good, honest 30mpg (9.5l/100km).

Considering its weight, the 220 Series performed admirably quickly, with 60mph (100km/h) showing on the speedometer from rest in slightly less than 13 seconds. At about the same time, BMW was heading at a similarly brisk pace for financial oblivion; the Munich company would be back, though.

Trans-Stuttgart-Mission

The Cisitalia Grand Prix car, designed after the war by Porsche for wealthy Italian industrialist Piero Dusio, included permanent four-wheel drive. A 1.5-litre V12, the car resembled a scaled-down pre-war Auto-Union, also designed by Porsche, but one of its cleverest features was the all-synchromesh five-speed gearbox – the brainchild of Porsche's transmission expert Leopold Schmid.

As Ferry Porsche observed in his autobiography, *Cars Are My Life*, 'The development of this ring synchronization system to the series production stage was a costly business, but it led in the end to the production of a gearbox that was to be used by many important companies.'

Rear suspension was independent by swing axles, a system that provoked a tide of protest over the years. Those who complained about 'tricky' on-the-limit handling were usually in need of driving tuition.

This hub assembly – from a later car with rear disc brakes – illustrates the extent to which the cars from Stuttgart were 'over-engineered'. Virtually every component was bullet-proof and capable of enduring beyond the call of duty. When the crunch does come, remedial work is usually expensive.

Porsche put its new gearbox into production with the 356 coupé from 1951; a similar system was used by Mercedes-Benz on the W196 Grand Prix car in 1954. It worked so well that many European manufacturers, including Daimler-Benz, adopted the synchromesh design for their production models. By the beginning of the 1960s, the vast majority of European production cars had synchromesh manual gearboxes, but the increasing trend in North America towards a preference for automatics naturally led to Mercedes, and others, to follow the same route.

The original automatic option fitted to these cars was not especially successful or popular. Known as the Hydrak clutch system, it was a semi-auto in which the driver operated the gear lever in the normal manual way, but did so without the use of a clutch pedal. Discontinued towards the end of 1961, the Hydrak was replaced by a fully automatic system developed by Daimler-Benz. A four-speeder, this increased the luxury appeal of the range, and was regarded as having novelty value.

Of the four-speed epicyclic type, with a fluid coupling, the auto gearbox was not up to Detroit standards, but represented a fair effort all the same. According to *Autocar*, 'In general, the changes are unobtrusive, the exception being the full-throttle kick-down; on the test car one was discouraged from using this anyhow, since the physical effort needed was heavy.'

The two penalties for auto transmission were, of course, fuel consumption and performance, both of which suffered slightly in comparison with manual counterparts.

Interestingly, some also found fault with the regular manual-change cars. *The Motor*, for example, noted that 'a replacement gearbox on our car was probably too new to be at its best and the change was not one to repay a forceful, heavy-handed driver; the harder the baulk-ring synchromesh is pressed, the harder it resists, giving the impression of a heavy, sticky action. On the other hand, with gentle, deliberate movements and a steady pressure, the lever slips through with ease and precision, although not particularly quickly.'

Naturally, the criticism was relative. People had come to expect nothing short of perfection from Daimler-Benz, and for the most part they got it. For the slickest gear changes, and completely 'bullet-proof' gearboxes at this time, the VW Beetle remained unsurpassed.

Independence of a Kind

While many argue that the old Brooklands racing track in Surrey in the south-east of England was responsible for stunting chassis development in the British motor industry, the Nürburgring did just the opposite for German car makers.

During the 1950s, the cars from Porsche,

Volkswagen and Daimler-Benz were equipped with all-round independent suspension, while many British cars soldiered on with 'solid' rear axles well into the 1960s.

At the front the Fintails utilized unequal-length transverse wishbones with coil springs and anti-roll bar, while the rear set-up was similar to the system used on the 300SL Roadstern (production of which ended in 1963). Much criticized, and much misunderstood, the rear comprised single-joint low-pivot swing axles with coil springs and additional compensating spring.

During the 1930s, when the rear-engined Auto-Union GP cars ran with swing-axle rear suspension, an abundance of power frequently saw these fabulous machines step out of line in the normal post-Vintage manner. Unfortunately, the skilled antics of drivers such as Bernd Rosemeyer, Tazio Nuvolari and Hans Stuck were interpreted by some misguided journalists as meaning that the rear suspension was inherently flawed in some way. Their inaccurate criticisms were often repeated over the years, clearly showing how they had failed to see how well thought out the Fintail was.

Predictably, the rear suspension was 'softened' to take account of American taste – the cars frequently 'bottomed out' on events like the East African Safari Rally – but the handling and roadholding were predictable and safe. *The Motor*'s 1961 road test revealed some body roll and tyre squeal under hard cornering, which was to be expected with a car in this class. The report's writer added the following:

> On fast, winding roads the car is delightful to drive or ride in, giving a feeling of safety which derives partly from the absence of the rocking motion

Opposite *Introduced in 1961, the 4-cylinder cars were distinguished externally by single circular headlamps. Economical, dependable 'sloggers', they were built to the same standard as the 6-cylinder cars.*

which some vehicles suffer when cornered fast and partly from the ability of the suspension to absorb almost any kind of road surface without noticeable effect on the roadholding.

The same magazine reported initial understeer, turning into oversteer if the car was pushed too hard, and advised hard braking before a corner to prevent the swing axles from travelling completely through their arcs. (The reporter had clearly never learned the art of opposite-lock motoring; this is all it takes to bring any car with swing axles back on to an even keel!) Ride quality was adjudged to be exceptional, although many argued that Jaguars and Rolls-Royces were superior in this respect (despite their ability frequently to induce a feeeling of queasiness in rear-seat passengers).

For the steering mechanism Daimler-Benz adhered to its tried and tested recirculating ball,

with the added bonus of a steering damper. At 3.5 turns from lock to lock it was high-geared, but gave an impression of even higher gearing thanks to the large diameter of the steering wheel. By the standards of the day, the steering felt direct and precise, but somewhat vague and ponderous by comparison with modern Mercs. With 13in diameter wheels, unsprung weight was reduced over the more conventional 15in items, but 7.25 × 13 crossply tyres did little ultimately to inspire confidence when approaching the limit of road adhesion.

The company's chief development engineer Rudi Uhlenhaut was instrumental in encouraging tyre companies to improve their technology. Development of radial tyres began in the mid-1950s and, by the time they had been virtually perfected, in 1963, their superiority became immediately apparent. The 230SL 'Pagoda' Mercedes-Benz, shod with the new

The 4-cylinder cars had considerably less external brightwork than the more expensive 6-cylinder version, and arguably looked all the better for this treatment. They were also 2in (50mm) shorter in length.

radials, proved itself to be as quick on a twisty race track as a 3-litre Ferrari.

Braking was arguably the only area of car design in which German engineers lagged well behind their British counterparts, and in this respect Mercedes was no exception. Dunlop had developed disc brakes for aeroplanes during the war, and worked closely with Jaguar during the late 1940s and early 50s. Both the C- and D-Types were particularly successful in high-profile sports-car events such as Le Mans – Jaguar won the classic 24 Hours five times in the 1950s – while Mercedes and Porsche soldiered on doggedly with drums.

Four-cylinder cars, particularly the diesel versions, furthered the company's reputation for reliability and longevity, but performance was never more than adequate.

The range-topping 3-litre 300SE was an expensive addition to the range in 1961. This advanced car boasted air-suspension, servo-assisted brakes and steering and automatic transmission.

Fintails were equipped with the 9.05in diameter Alfin-type turbo-finned drums, which were about as good as drums brakes got. *The Motor* reported that they were very light in use, and gave sufficient cooling in British weather to obviate fade during heavy use. Unevenness and slight judder at low speeds, however, were observed after hard braking from 90mph (145km/h) to a standstill.

Moving On

By the autumn of 1961 Daimler-Benz, along with the rest of the civilized automotive world, was ready to move on. This new decade would finally see the burial of the stodge of the 1950s. Exciting new cars included Jaguar's E-Type, Mercedes' own 230SL and the Porsche 911 (from 1963-4), all equipped with lusty 6-cylinder engines and pleasing looks. The performance of these cars alone was suf-

ficient evidence of growing affluence among the emergent middle class.

Daimler-Benz was heading in much the same direction in which it had headed since the company began making cars after the war. Top-notch saloons and fine Grand Tourers had always been on the agenda but, from 1961, the range began to expand for the benefit of a wider audience.

One Up, Two Down

Some regarded the launch of the E-Type Jaguar in 1961 as some kind of automotive milestone. The car was not only aesthetically pleasing, but also offered Ferrari-like performance at a snip. The press concentrated its efforts on the new car, especially in Britain, and other new releases were almost glossed over – but not quite.

Important new cars in the Fintail line-up at this time included a flagship, the 300SE, and the long-promised 4-cylinder cars – the 190 and 190D. By any standards, the 300SE was a superb piece of equipment and, like all Mercedes flagships over the years, ownership was the preserve of those with a few bob to spare. In Britain, for example, the 300SE retailed at almost £4,000, roughly twice the price of Jaguar's E-Type. The initial difficulty for Daimler-Benz lay in making the 300SE look sufficiently different from the less glamorous cars in the range. No one who bought one of these magnificent cars wished to be confused with the German taxi drivers who formed a very long queue for the diesel-engined 190D.

In the fashion of the day, the 300SE was quite dressed up. Apart from 300SE badging at the rear, there was additional brightwork around the wheel arches, across the flanks, around the D-pillar vents and along the sills. But, although it was kitted out with state-of-the-art luxuries, the 300SE's greatest asset arguably lay in its 3-litre 6-cylinder engine. Previous versions of this engine had powered the 300SL to victory in the 1952 Le Mans 24 Hours, and had served particularly well in the 300SL Gullwing and Roadster road cars. The 300SE's unit differed, however, in that both the cylinder head and block were made of aluminium-alloy. This reduced weight by 75lb (35kg), although the car was still 4cwt heavier than the 220S and 220SE models.

With Bosch mechanical fuel injection, identical to the system used on the 220SE, maximum power output of 160bhp was sufficient for a top speed of 107.2mph (171.5km/h) (according to *The Motor's* 1963 report). The same publication also recorded overall fuel consumption of 13.4mpg (21.1l/100km), and a 0–50mph (0–80km/h) capability of 7.9 seconds. Allied to the standard automatic gearbox – a manual was later offered as an option – the car also achieved the standing quarter-mile in 18.2 seconds, and 0–100mph (0–160km/h) in 37 seconds which, for a heavy 'limo' with the aerodynamic properties of two men in a wardrobe, gave rise to the idea that this was really a sporting saloon for sybarites.

From the armchair-like seats, *The Motor's* testers discovered that 'the heavy doors shut with the right sort of damped thud, the floor is heavily carpeted, the upholstery is genuine leather and the sealing and soundproofing produce that feeling of being shut off from the noise of the outside world.

Criticism was confined to the facia and combination speedometer – 'much the worst feature' – and to mechanical noise from the engine, presumed to be a 'by-product' of its all-alloy architecture. Of this the report's writer made the following remarks:

> Inside the car this penetrated as a subdued, efficient and not unpleasant under-bonnet whirr at moderate speeds but towards the maxima in the intermediate gears the noise became obtrusive. In top gear also it is audible at high cruising speeds but this is largely attributable to the remarkable silence of the car in other respects; even at 100mph [160km/h] wind noise is practically negligible, a characteristic which few other cars can match or even approach.

Power-assisted steering, air-conditioning and servo-assisted Dunlop disc brakes at all four corners were fitted as standard, and few found fault with any of these features. The real novelty, though, was the air-suspension system. This was not new in the industry – both Cadillac and Citroën had attempted (with varying degrees of success) to improve upon conventional springing media – and it was almost inevitable that Mercedes would also follow this route.

Built to a Daimler-Benz design, the suspension used rubber air bags, maintained under pressure by a pump that was belt-driven from the crankshaft. Each bag was automatically linked and, with correction valves above each, the whole system was self-levelling. Front and rear anti-roll bars ensured that the 'sogginess' inherent in an 'ungoverned' air-suspension system was largely absent.

Naturally, the system was complex and,

190c (W110) 1961–65

Body style	Four–door saloon

Engine

Cylinders	4
Bore × stroke	85mm × 83.6mm
Capacity	1897cc
Timing	Single-overhead camshaft
Compression ratio	8.7:1
Carburettor	Single Solex 34 PJCB
Max power	80bhp at 5,000rpm
Max torque	105lb ft at 2,500rpm

Transmission

Gearbox	Synchromesh 4-speed

Ratios

First	4.05:1
Second	2.28:1
Third	1.53:1
Fourth	1:1
Reverse	4.05:1

Automatic transmission optional from August 1962

Ratios

First	3.98:1
Second	2.52:1
Third	1.58:1
Fourth 1:1	
Reverse	4.15:1

Final-drive 4.08:1 or optional 4.10:1

Suspension and steering

Front	Wishbones, coil springs and anti-roll bar
Rear	Low-pivot swinging axles with coil springs, mechanical compensating spring and telescopic dampers
Steering	Daimler-Benz recirculating ball
Wheels	Pressed-steel 5.5J×13

Brakes	Servo-assisted drums all round. Front discs from August 1963

Dimensions

Track	(front) 58in (1450mm) (rear) 58.5in (1462.5mm)
Wheelbase	106.3in (2657.5mm)
Overall length	186.5in (4662.5mm)
Overall width	70.7in (1767.5mm)
Overall height	58.8in (1470mm)

although failures of the pneumatics were rare, the suspension was generously supported by rubber buffers. Its complexity also bumped up the cost of owning the car, but Mercedes' engineers rarely shied away from innovative technology merely on the grounds of expense.

Ride quality and high-speed stability were of the highest order, rivalling the best of the rest. *The Motor* had this to say about the road-holding:

> The Mercedes takes fast corners in impeccable style maintaining a slight understeer, rolling only moderately and displaying the indifference to bumpy road surfaces that one expects with first-class independent suspension all round. On slow corners it naturally feels a little clumsier but it can be thrown around very much more vigorously than most cars of comparable size before the tyres squeal. On ice and snow, however, traction is not particularly good in spite of a self-limiting differential and because of the automatic transmission and good soundproofing the driver is often unaware that the wheels are spinning until the tail moves sideways.

Allied to the air-suspension system was a clever innovation that aided stability, particularly under braking. At the rear the brake calipers were connected to forward-projecting torque arms, which effectively prevented the tail lifting when braking. In effect, this negated the tendency of the swing axles to 'arch', and contributed to an extremely safe-handling vehicle.

Without doubt, the 220SE was representative of considerable technical advancement in production-car engineering. The majority of its 'new' technical wonders had been tried before, either on competition cars, or on the road cars of comparable rivals, but few manufacturers had successfully combined so many worthwhile features in one package.

A Rolls-Royce Silver Cloud cost nearly twice as much as a 300SE, while the relatively unsophisticated Rover 3-litre was consider-

ably less; in reality, the Mercedes was, all told, the pick of the bunch. Not everyone warmed to Mercedes styling, but Daimler-Benz were just about big enough to consider that this was not their problem.

Concluding its report on the 300SE, *The Motor*'s final comment was that 'in several respects they [Daimler-Benz] have not reached the highest current standards but in building a large and extremely comfortable car with steering, roadholding and handling which would be creditable in a car of half the weight, they have had outstanding success.'

Four in Front

Production of the 190 and 190D 4-cylinder Fintails (W110) began in June 1961, providing direct replacements for the outgoing 180 and 180D Pontons. 'Entry-level' cars intended to serve taxi drivers, family motorists, fleet buyers and those who could take no more of BMW 'bubblecar' motoring, the 190s were the 'sensible shoes' of the West German motor industry.

A middle-class conveyance, the 190 was neither stylish nor pretty, but it did hold the trump cards of reliability, durability and almost unrivalled safety. Although similar in appearance to the 6-cylinder cars, the 'fours' differed in that they sat on a shorter wheelbase, and were 2in (50mm) shorter in the nose.

In place of the *Lichtenheiten* (stacked headlamps), there were circular lights, similar to those used on the Pontons, separate indicators below the headlamps, and single-bladed bumpers. Slightly less brightwork – the flanks and 'D' pillars were unadorned – went against the grain of contemporary trends but, with the benefit of hindsight, this was a distinct advantage from an aesthetic viewpoint.

In all respects, the car was unmistakably from the Mercedes mould. Built to withstand the driving antics of an Italian with a grievance – the ultimate benchmark test of durability – the 190 was a high-quality, if pedestrian, work-

300SE (W112) long-wheelbase saloon 1961–65

Specification as for 220SEb except for the following:

Engine

Cylinders	6
Bore × stroke	85mm × 88mm
Capacity	2996cc
Fuel system	Bosch mechanical fuel injection
Timing	Single-overhead camshaft
Compression ratio	8.7:1
Max power	160bhp at 5,000rpm
Max torque	185lb ft at 3,800rpm

Transmission
Ratios

First	4.05:1
Second	2.28:1
Third	1.53:1
Fourth	1:1
Reverse	4.15:1

Automatic
Ratios

First	3.98:1
Second	2.52:1
Third	1.58:1
Fourth	1:1

2503 (W100) 1965–69

Unitary construction 4-door saloon

Engine

Cylinders	6
Bore × stroke	82mm × 78.8mm
Capacity	2496cc
Timing	Single-overhead camshaft
Compression ratio	9:1
Carburettor	2 Zenith 35/40 INAT
Max power	130bhp at 5,400rpm
Max torque	143lb ft at 4,000rpm

Transmission

Gearbox	4-speed manual with synchromesh

Ratios

First	4.05:1
Second	2.23:1
Third	1.42:1
Fourth	1:1

Automatic

First	3.98:1
Second	2.52:1
Third	1.58:1
Fourth	1:1
Final-drive	3.92:1

Suspension and steering

Front	Transverse wishbones, coil springs and anti-roll bar
Rear with	Low-pivot swing-axle coil springs, compensating spring and telescopic dampers
Steering	Daimler-Benz recirculating ball

Brakes

	Servo-assisted discs all round

Dimensions

Track	(front) 58.3in (1457.5mm) (rear) 58.5in (1462.5mm)
Wheelbase	108.3in (2707.5mm)
Overall length	192.9in (4822.5mm)
Overall width	71.3in (1782.5mm)
Overall height	56.7in (1417.5mm)

horse and appreciated for this reason on almost every continent.

The cabin was capable of accommodating five adults in reasonable comfort, and the boot was sufficiently large for a 'ton' of luggage, or several naughty children.

The interior was spoilt by the hideous speedometer, a piece of design that must have warmed the hearts of those working on the BMW 1500 saloon at this time. (Incidentally, allthough BMW had plans to make capital out of Daimler-Benz's 'mistakes', it soon became clear that all was not well in Munich in 1961. BMW had been rescued by Quandt money but, having rushed its first new saloon

250SE (W108) 1965–68	
Specification as for 250S except as follows:	
Engine	
Cylinders	6
Bore × stroke	82mm × 78.8mm
Capacity	2496cc
Compression ratio	9.3:1
Fuel sustem	Bosch fuel injection
Max power	150bhp at 5,500rpm
Max torque	159lb ft at 4,200rpm

300SE (W108) 1965–67	
Engine	
Cylinders	6
Bore × stroke	85mm × 88mm
Capacity	2996cc
Compression ratio	8.8:1
Fuel system	Bosch mechanical fuel injection
Max power	170bhp at 5,400rpm
Max torque	183lb ft at 4,000rpm

into production, started out with what one senior BMW marketing man described rather bluntly as a 'shit car'. Daimler-Benz had never been in the business of building 'shit cars', and it would be a long time before BMW would be able to compete on equal terms with Stuttgart.)

Obviously, the 190 followed in the wake of its refined, 6-cylinder sisters. The fact that it bore a very close resemblance to the more expensive cars in the range was no

coincidence. Daimler-Benz had successfully used the same ploy in 1954 with the 190SL, a car that closely resembled the brutally expensive, and wickedly fast, 300SL Gullwing. Unlike the Gullwing, the 190SL was moderately profitable for the company, and this was just one reason why the same basic engine that propelled the 'baby' sports car was used, in various states of tune, in both the 1950s Pontons and the 4-cylinder Fintails.

A long-wheelbase version of the 220D and 230 appeared in 1967, intended as competition for the Volkswagen Kombi. Seven- and eight-seaters were available and justifiably popular with taxi drivers, airport authorities and hoteliers.

230S (W111) 1965–68 saloon	
Specification as for 220b except for the following:	
Engine	
Cylinders	6
Bore × stroke	82mm × 72.8mm
Capacity	2281cc
Compression ratio	9:1
Carburettor	2 Zenith 35/40 INAT downdraught carburettors
Max power	120bhp at 5,400rpm
Max torque	132lb ft at 4,000rpm
Transmission	
Ratios	
First	4.05:1
Second	2.23:1
Third	1.41:1
Fourth	1:1

Fintail estates were intended as rugged utility vehicles; as such, the majority led an exceptionally hard life and are now relatively rare.

Developing a respectable 80bhp, the 1897cc unit was no more powerful than the engine that served the Ponton but, thanks to a higher compression ratio and improved carburation, it was more lively up through the gears. It could cruise comfortably at 80mph (125km/h), and top 95mph (150km/h). Its nearest and natural rival came from Sweden in the form of the Volvo 'Amazon' series, but it was the Merc that gained global recognition.

The success of the diesel-engined version was even more extraordinary. Fitted with a revised 2-litre version of Mercedes' ubiquitous 'oil-burner', the 190D pushed

Above *The styling of the estate was not especially successful, though it was characteristic of the period.*

Below *Like all fads, the fins that gave the cars their nickname disappeared quickly and discreetly. By the mid-1960s, Mercedes considered that this 'deviation' had been a mistake, and quickly returned to less conspicuous styling.*

out a paltry, but adequate, 55bhp. To criticize the diesel version on the grounds of performance, however, was to miss the point. Without exception, all diesel-engined vehicles during this era were noisy, smelly contraptions. Their main redeeming feature was good fuel mileage. The diesel Merc became (and remains) the staple of German taxi drivers, although some consider that BMW's efforts in this direction during the 1990s resulted in superior machines.

Progress through Pressure

In 1963, the company launched the 'Pagoda' 230SL, introduced a long-wheelbase version of the 300SE, and fitted disc brakes to the front of the 190, 190D and 220. Despite their popularity in both mainland Europe and North America, the first-generation Fintails lived a relatively short production life. By the early 1960s, the fashion for the fintail styling that had been so popular in the USA had passed. It was odd that Mercedes had followed others - virtually unique in the company's history. Volkswagen's chief executive, Heinz Nordhoff, was proved to have been right all along in keeping faith with one established model – the increasingly successful Beetle.

In 1964, the 220S was treated to revised Zenith carburettors, and the 300SE had its compression ratio raised to give an extra 10bhp. The latter also got a high-geared final-drive ratio of 3.75:1 to increase its top speed to 125mph (200km/h) (the same, incidentally, as that of the 3.5-litre V8 MGB sports car of the 1970s).

Power-assisted steering – something of a luxury on saloons at this time – was standard on the 4-cylinder cars from 1964 but, to all intents and purposes, it was all over for the first generation by the autumn of 1965.

Fintails 2

Because Mercedes had always produced a range of cars of similar quality, customers from the bottom to the top could always be assured that they would get the best in engineering integrity. There was a particular problem with this otherwise laudable policy – those who forked out a huge sum for a range-topper were rewarded with few outward signs that their car was from the top drawer. Overt displays of wealth and prestige were part and parcel of the 1960s, and Mercedes needed to go along with customer demands. The saloon range was divided into two distinct types. Launched at the 1965 Frankfurt Motor Show, the new range (codenamed W108) comprised 250S, 250SE, 300SE and the long-wheelbase 300SEL. All had 6-cylinder engines of 2.5 litres or above.

At the other end of the scale, the 200 and 200D replaced the 190 Series, there was a 230 instead of a 220, and a 230S in place of the 220S. In addition, there was a mid-range 230, with the regular short-nose body, fitted with a 6-cylinder engine.

While the 230S and more expensive models were equipped with the distinctive *Lichtenheiten* headlamps, the 200, 200D and 230 had revised and much larger lamp clusters, comprising fog lamps, parking lights and indicators, below the main headlamps. Additional chrome trim and improved seats were part of the revised Fintail package, along with engine developments. The 2-litre diesel still only developed 55bhp, but there were five main crankshaft bearings instead of three, and the unit ran appreciably more smoothly as a result.

The 200's petrol engine, increased in capacity from 1897cc to 1988cc, was also treated to five main bearings, and benefited from an increase in power – up from 80bhp to 90bhp. Both the 230 and 230S were equipped with the 2.3-litre 6-cylinder engine, and instead of the 230SL sports car's Bosch fuel-injection system, there were Solex carburettors for the standard 230 and Zeniths for the 230S.

The cars on the lower rung were not as plushly equipped as they might have been, but this was a deliberate ploy to ensure that the 250S, and other cars in the new S-Class range, retained an aura of luxury and exclusivity.

For the 1967 model year, two further additions to the Fintail range included a spacious estate car and a 7-seater version of the 200D. The latter, which was some 26in (650mm) longer than the standard 200D, was designed with an extra row of seats in the middle of the car. Aimed squarely at people engaged in ferrying passengers to and from airports, it was a supremely practical, if ungainly, vehicle.

With 308lb (140kg) of extra weight in its bodyshell, the standard 2-litre diesel engine was frequently stretched to the limit, especially with a full complement of passengers aboard. Porsche had once built tractors that were quicker off the mark, and the poor old 'limo's' top speed of around 78mph (125km/h) was unrealistic with seven people aboard. Unsurprisingly, production lasted just nine months.

Both revised classes of cars sold extremely well, despite the dip in the German economy in the mid-1960s. Year-on-year sales increased dramatically, but the huge success enjoyed by Daimler-Benz was due not only to the improvements on the new cars. Porsche, Volkswagen and BMW were also selling more and more vehicles, and investing heavily in new production facilities merely to keep pace with a world that was increasingly hungry for cars. Access to financial credit was greater than it ever had been, and western economies had climbed away from post-war austerity to hitherto unknown levels of affluence.

Opposite *Throughout the 1960s, Mercs were Europe's most coveted, prestigious and finest saloons. By 1968, however, BMW was poised to challenge this position, and Daimler-Benz would be forced to work even harder.*

2 The Coupés, Cabriolets and 600s

The Luxury Market

In the 1920s, after a number of years of motorists being battered by the wind and rain in open-top vehicles, the idea of a stylish, luxury motor car evolved. In the early years of motoring, the vast majority of cars had no roof; on those that did have one, the roof was of the most rudimentary kind. With the advent of enclosed saloons in the 1920s, designers and coachbuilders began increasingly to look at ways in which the self-indulgent motorist could be more generously accommodated.

Daimler-Benz, Rolls-Royce, Horch, Bugatti, Alfa Romeo, and many others, worked industriously to produce carriages of great distinction and elegance. The inspired designers at Bugatti produced what was arguably the greatest of all the luxury cars. The Type 41 Royale was expensive, beautiful and extraordinary, intended for use by kings and queens, and limited to just half a dozen examples – but it was a financial disaster. After some months of head-scratching, Ettore Bugatti finally came to terms with the view that extreme cars were not a great idea. A sensible compromise emerged with the Type 46, the 'Baby Royale', which was more affordable and considerably more successful.

With a long history of producing elitest machines, Daimler-Benz also decided in the 1960s to turn its hand once again to a top-

Introduced in 1961, the elegant coupe and cabriolet versions of the 'cooking' saloons enjoyed an unusually long production run of ten years. They were expensive, luxurious and beautifully engineered. Paul Bracq's timeless design dated from 1957, and reflects an age emerging from austerity.

All two-door coupes and cabriolets were fitted with 6-cylinder engines, and made for superb Grand Touring cars. Few machines of the 1960s ate motorway miles with the same degree of refinement. Note that the tail fins were slightly 'flattened'.

class breed. In terms of understated elegance, the two-door W111 and W112 coupés and cabriolets were without peer, and remain as coveted today as they were when they were first released.

Neither could Daimler-Benz resist the challenge of building its own version of Bugatti's Royale. A technical tour de force, bristling with state-of-the-art technology, the 600 was astounding in every way. Although it was considerably more successful than Bugatti's flop, the *Grosser* Mercedes also proved to be something of a questionable decision.

Peerless and Pillarless

For a talented designer, the main difficulty of the exhausting task of coming up with a new motor cars lies not in transcribing the imagination on to paper to produce a thing of great beauty, but in keeping the imagination within the parameters of what is practicable. The great French designer Paul Bracq was an acknowledged maestro in this field, and Daimler-Benz was lucky enough to have his name on the payroll.

By 1957, the W110/111/112 four-door saloons, which would replace the Pontons, had virtually taken shape on the drawing board. At roughly the same time, Bracq began outline sketches for a coupé version of the saloon, with pillarless doors. Much of the body was to have the same outline as the saloon, particularly at the rear, but the front end was much lower and sleeker. The large windscreen was of the 'wraparound' variety, much in vogue among American designers.

During 1958, Bracq's design work was turned into reality, appearing in slightly modified form to bring it closer to the production cars. The standard radiator from the 220SE was as inevitable as the star motif that sat on the top of it. There were *Lichtenheiten* too, of course, but the tailfins were considerably less 'fin-like', having been 'flattened' along their top surface. Both the coupé and cabriolet used the same floorpan as the saloon, but their bodies were wider and longer. With their rounded curves, their elegance by comparison with the rather angular saloon was undeniable. The inevitable strengthening panels in both bodies added a weight penalty, but this was a small

45

Above *Cabriolet versions had the advantage of four seats capable of accommodating adults of the fullest proportions. In some ways these cars were reminiscent of the great pre-war Mercedes cabriolets – Teutons with purpose, aimed at an elite incapable of accepting mediocrity.*

Left *Despite the immense strength of the cabriolet's 'A' pillars, they were not so wide that all-round visibility was impaired. Note the elegance of the hinge near the top of the quarter-light.*

Below *In time-honoured fashion, the rear side windows slid neatly into the quarter panel. With the window closed, the soft-top was a very good fit.*

price to pay for a car with such outstanding aesthetic value.

For such a large five-seater it was reasonable to expect that the cabriolet version would suffer from 'scuttle-shake' and flexing, but there was none. Even after many thousands of miles of hard use, the doors would continue to open and close perfectly – a sure sign that Daimler-Benz had done their homework properly.

The cabriolet's soft-top was very much in the German style of the day – of traditional three-tier 'sandwich' construction, it tucked neatly away behind the rear seats – but its rear window was, curiously, made of plastic and therefore vulnerable to scratching. (The Volkswagen Beetle was the only production car with a glass rear window, and this remained the case for many years!)

While there was some justifiable criticism over the layout of the standard saloon's interior, no one had cause to moan about the inside of the cabriolet and coupé. High-quality carpeting lay on the floor, Tex vinyl was used for the seat covers (or leather at extra cost), and every fixture and fitting was 'over-engineered' to the point of being indestructible.

Top right *The cabriolet's 'double-skinned' soft-top was fully lined, but 'cheapened' by the presence of a plastic rear window. Ironically, the world's only cabriolet with a glass rear window at this time was the Volkswagen Beetle.*

The soft-top was 'skirted' by a sturdy piece of stainless steel with studs attached for securing the cover when in the 'down' position.

*Leather-clad luxury
combined with polished
wood veneer in the
cabriolet created one of the
best driving environments
among Grand Tourers.
Seat comfort was without
parallel.*

*Many argue that the
quality of the wood veneer
used by Mercedes was not
up to the standards
insisted upon by Jaguar
and Rolls-Royce.*

Circular instruments flanked the central combination gauge, and could be clearly read through the gargantuan steering wheel. The layout of the instruments and controls was similar to that of the 300SL Roadster, and none the worse for this, but some criticized the instrumentation for being aesthetically dull.

Below *Massive external seat hinges were emulated by BMW, and look like a crude after-thought in comparison with their modern counterparts.*

Inspiration for the dashboard came from the mighty 300SL sports car, with a rectangular combination gauge flanked by two circular instruments – a tachometer on the left and a speedometer on the right (*see above*). All three instruments were enclosed in polished wood veneer, and black leather featured on the upper surface of the dashboard, to give an overall effect of virtually unrivalled opulence.

By contrast, the steering wheel was not a success, typically on the large side of 'sensible'. The two spokes were cited so low as to appear ugly, the chromed horn ring obscured the instruments when turning left or right, and the padded central boss simply looked incongruous. The wheel's saving grace was that it was at least pleasant to use.

From the driving seat the cars felt every bit as good as they looked. Their sheer solidity and weight inspired confidence, and an overwhelming sense of safety. Interestingly, original or well-restored examples have a rather modern feel today, which indicates how advanced the cars were for their time.

Superbly styled alloy wheels were available as extra-cost options from 1969, and many owners fitted earlier cars with them retrospectively. The same style of alloy wheel was also available for contemporary SL sports cars.

Down Under

Mechanically, the cars were similar to their saloon counterparts, differing only in relatively unimportant detail. The 220SE's fuel-injection 2195cc engine was mated to a choice of the four-speed manual or four-speed automatic transmission. Despite the additional weight of the coupé and cabriolet, performance was similar to that of the saloon, although the coupé felt slightly less lively through the gears. A top speed of 105mph (170km/h) was easily achieved. Naturally, the inferior aerodynamics of the cabriolet with the soft-top down restricted its top speed, but this did not matter a jot. The cabriolet was never intended as out-and-out sports machine, but as a touring car in the grandest of Mercedes traditions.

The suspension was similarly carried over from the saloon, but had a slightly lower ride height. In characteristic manner, ride was firm, though never harsh, and the roadholding was superb. Low-pivot swing axles were used at the rear and continued to be criticized in some quarters for a tendency to produce 'snap-out' oversteer at, or beyond, the limits of tyre adhesion. This did not bother skilled drivers, who knew the techniques to employ at the limit.

Continuing reliance on swing-axle rear suspension resulted in tedious press criticism. The system worked extremely well, and gave ample notice that the rear end was on the brink of stepping out of line, but journalists still called for improvement.

Sales figures support the view that few customers were prepared to take notice of swing-axle prophets of doom. Between 1961 and 1962, sales nearly doubled – from 2,537 to 4,287 units – and Daimler-Benz banked healthy profits.

Jaguar certainly stole the 1961 Geneva Motor Show with the E-Type, but this 149-mph (240-km/h) two-seater sports car was aimed at a different audience, and provided little in the way of real competition for the Mercedes.

And Then There Were Three

The majority of 220SE coupé and cabriolet owners were satisfied with their lot, but most would have welcomed a more powerful engine to propel the extra weight. In the spring of 1962 Daimler-Benz duly obliged, and debuted the expensive 300SE in coupé and cabriolet guises. The all-alloy 'six', which also saw service in the last few production versions of the 300SL Roadster, was an obvious choice.

Although criticized by some for its level of mechanical noise at high speed, this lusty power unit was among the true classics in every sense. Although the automatic was slightly slower than the manual, both versions were capable of around 120mph (195km/h) depending upon the choice of final-drive ratios. By any standards of the day this was a fast motor car. By way of comparison, Porsche's contemporary 1.6-litre 356C – a pukka sports car – was capable of 115mph (185km/h). Daimler-Benz narrowly missed shooting itself in the foot with this car, because the company's own 230SL, which was not a sports car in the accepted sense, was also slightly slower than the 3-litre coupés and cabriolets.

Naturally, such performance in a heavy car did not come cheap and the 3-litres were expensive both to buy and to run. Fuel consumption was rarely better than 20mpg

(14l/100km), although this was comparable to other luxury cars of its ilk, and in any case the subject would not become a serious issue until the 1973 Middle East oil crisis.

Munich Challenges

The advent of the 300SE, a true flagship of the saloon range, left something of a gulf between this car and the original 220SE, which is why the latter was replaced by the 2.5-litre 250SE in 1965. With 150bhp, it was fast but the engine's great strength lay in its improved durability.

With a vast motorway network at their disposal, German drivers were able to cut inter-city journey times simply by pressing the throttle pedal to the floor and holding it there. The lucky ones made time savings that would have been unimaginable a few earlier, while others ended up sitting on the *autobahn* hard shoulder in a pool of oil, peering down a long bonnet at a smouldering radiator.

Although Mercedes had used chromium-plated piston rings for some time, normal wear and tear could result in scored bores. Chief development engineer Rudi Uhlenhaut therefore sought a tougher coating material and settled for molybdenum. With a melting point of 2550 degrees centigrade – 1000 degrees higher than chromium – it proved much more resistant to wear, and virtually solved previous problems overnight.

The other major improvement was the introduction of a seven-bearing crankshaft. The long 78.8mm stroke demanded greater resistance to the natural forces of reciprocation, the new crankshaft also leading to a power unit that was inherently smoother in operation. To prevent valve-bounce from constant over-revving, the nose of the crankshaft was fitted with a large damper, making the engine safe up to a maximum of 7,000rpm.

With Bosch fuel injection there was 174lb ft of torque at 4,500rpm, giving a

250SE (W111) 1965–67

Specification as for 220SE coupé and convertible except for the following:

Engine
Cylinders	6
Bore × stroke	82mm × 78.8mm
Capacity	2496cc
Compression ratio	9.3:1
Max power	150bhp at 5,500rpm
Max torque	159lb ft at 4,200rpm

Transmission
Ratios
First	4.05:1
Second	2.23:1
Third	1.42:1
Fourth	1:1
Final-drive	3.92:1

10 per cent gain over the 2.5-litre carburettor engine fitted to the standard saloon.

These mechanical developments ran parallel with similar changes to the SL sports cars, the 250SL arriving on stream from 1965.

Outwardly the 250SE was distinguishable by its chromed boot-lid badge, and 14in wheels fitted with wide, chromed wheel trims, but in most other respects the car was unchanged. All-round disc brakes improved stopping power tremendously, and finally welcomed the upper echelons of the Mercedes range into the modern world. BMW's 2.5-litre 525i has outsold the 3-litre 530i in more modern times; for the same reason, the 250SE ate into the popularity of its 3-litre sister. The large differential in price between the two cars could hardly justify the relatively small gap in performance, and the complexities of the 300SE had not endeared themselves to the 'Sunday-morning' do-it-yourself experts, either.

The 2778cc 6-cylinder engine in the 280SE developed a respectable 160bhp at 5,500rpm. A robust power unit, it lacked only the smoothness of similar-capacity engines from BMW in the late 1960s.

280SE (W111) 1968–71

Specification as for 250SE coupé and convertible except for the following:

Engine
Cylinders	6
Bore × stroke	86.5mm × 78.8mm
Capacity	2778cc
Compression ratio	9.5:1
Max power	160bhp at 5,500rpm
Max torque	177lb ft at 4,250rpm

Transmission
Gearbox	5-speed manual optional from 1969

Ratios
First	3.96:1
Second	2.34:1
Third	1.43:1
Fourth	1:1
Fifth	0.87:1
Final-drive	3.69:1

Along with the 250SL sports car, the 250SE and 350SE coupé and cabriolet were replaced during 1967 by 2.8-litre cars. Badged as a 280SE, the revised 6-cylinder engine included a reprofiled camshaft and improved fuel-injection system, which genuinely improved the fuel consumption. An optional five-speed overdrive gearbox further improved fuel mileage in the upper rev range.

Just a year after the launch of the latest 'six', BMW challenged Stuttgart with a splendid range of saloons and coupés, also fitted with powerful 6-cylinder power units. It was no coincidence that, apart from the mid-range 2.5-litre Beemer, Munich's power units were also of 2.8-litre capacity. Competition between the two producers on the home market became fierce, in a gentlemanly sort of way, and both also began to fight harder for American sales.

No one really believed at this time that BMW would ever achieve anything but second-rate status to the people who had invented the motor car, but it was clear from the launch of the V8-engined 280SE 3.5 in 1969 that Daimler-Benz could not afford to sit on its corporate laurels. In North America, where the economy was booming in the late 1960s, the V8 reigned supreme, particularly among performance and luxury cars. Respected journals such as *Road & Track* and *Car & Driver* frequently described anything from Europe with a 3-litre 'six' as a 'medium-range' car.

In an attempt to be taken seriously in North America, Daimler-Benz put a fresh V8 into production, while BMW remained with its refined 6-cylinder cars. BMW, like Porsche many years previously, also began to invest heavily in motor sport, while the senior Stuttgart company, ever-mindful of Le Mans 1955, stayed resolutely away from the tracks.

With a bore and stroke of 92 × 65.8mm, the V8 had an overall capacity of 3499cc. With Bosch fuel injection and a relatively high compression ratio of 9.5:1, it developed 200bhp at

280SE 3.5 (W111) 1969–71

Specification as for 280SE coupé and convertible except for the following:

Engine
Cylinders	V8
Bore × stroke	92mm × 65.8mm
Capacity	3499cc
Timing	Single-overhead camshaft per bank
Compression ratio	9.5:1
Fuel system	Bosch electronic fuel injection
Max power	200bhp at 5,800rpm
Max torque	211lb ft at 4,000rpm

Transmission
Gear ratios	
First	3.96:1
Second	2.34:1
Third	1.46:1
Fourth	1:1
Reverse	3.71:1
5-speed gearbox optional	

5,500rpm, or 180bhp with the optional low-compression engine. With a top speed in the region of 125mph (200km/h), and the capability of accelerating from standstill to 60mph in 9.7secs, this was a mighty and impressive machine. Fuel consumption was in the region of 15mpg (19l/100km); in North America, where the price of gas was among the lowest in the world, this did not really matter. In Europe, where petrol was considerably more expensive, it was assumed that anyone sufficiently well-heeled to buy one of these cars would not object to sky-high fuel bills.

The one bugbear for all car manufacturers, however, was the increasingly stringent US legislation governing exhaust emissions. At first, engineers began to address these problems in the simplest possible manner. Low-compression pistons, exhaust-recirculation devices and retarded ignition all helped Californians in particular to breathe a little easier, but this had to be paid for in comparatively poor engine performance. Larger-capacity engines – Mercedes had a 4.5-litre engine waiting in the wings – would eventually answer the performance problem, but this would arrive too late for the classic SE coupés and cabriolets.

By 1971, they had run their course and were discontinued to make way for a more modern range. In principle and concept, these cars had been absolutely right for the 1960s. Elegant, powerful and purposeful, they embraced all the engineering tenets that Prof Porsche had 'dialled' into the cars he had designed for the company in the late 1920s and beyond.

For some, the 1960s was a heady decade of change, conflict and upheaval on a hitherto unknown scale. In the motoring world, Porsche revolutionized the concept of the

One of the most technically advanced cars of the 1960s, the 600 was a true limousine with every conceivable luxury, intended for heads of state. Its only serious rival was the Phantom V Rolls-Royce – preference was dictated by political allegiance.

sports-racing car in 1969 with the awe-inspiring 917. Despite the widely held view that the VW Beetle was dead, these remarkable cars were selling in record-breaking numbers. In 1968, BMW launched the definitive mid-range sports saloon – the 2002. During the same period, chief BMC designer Roy Haynes was in the early days of penning a contraption that would be launched in 1970 as the Morris Marina. In motor manufacturing, it seemed, Britain was on the way down, the Italians were enduring their usual highs and lows, French car makers had got the bit between their teeth, and the great German companies were clearly on the way up.

A *Grosser* Exaggeration

The Mercedes-Benz SSK Series of cars of the 1930s represented serious automotive self-indulgence – an extreme caricature of the motor car itself. No expense was spared in their creation, and the results were formidable. Almost impervious to corrosion by dint of the thickest possible metalwork, the *Grosser* Mercs

Two versions of the 600 were available: the five/six-seater with 124in (3150mm) wheelbase or the seven/eight-seater Pullman with 153.5in (3837.5mm) wheelbase. Both were extremely expensive to buy and run.

were powerful, and great symbols of power – the preferred transport of such men as Adolf Hitler and Hermann Goering.

Although the excesses of the SSK could not be sustained after the war (even the luxury 300, launched in 1951, was tame by comparison), there have always been small numbers of people who are prepared to pay for exaggera-tions of the motor car, irrespective of prevail-ing economic conditions. In Britain, the Phan-tom V Rolls Royce stood firmly at the top of the tree, built for people with a serious bank balance, including the Queen. Cadillac built cars of equal magnitude and expense. By the end of the 1950s, Daimler-Benz's board took a decision to enter this market once again.

Frontal styling of the 600 reflected prevailing Mercedes thinking, except that the proportions were larger.

600 (W100) 1964–81

Unitary construction long-wheelbase saloon

Engine

Cylinders	V8
Bore × stroke	103mm × 95mm
Capacity	6332cc
Timing	Single-overhead camshaft per bank
Compression ratio	9:1
Fuel system	Bosch mechanical fuel injection
Max power	250bhp at 4,000rpm
Max torque	369lb ft at 2,800rpm

Transmission

Gearbox	4-speed automatic
Gear ratios	3.98:1
Second	2.52:1
Third	1.58:1
Fourth	1:1
Reverse	4.15:1
Final-drive	3.23:1

Suspension

Front	Wishbones, air units, auxiliary rubber springs and telescopic dampers
Rear	Low-pivot swing-axles with air units, auxiliary springs and telescopic dampers
Steering	Servo-assisted recirculating ball

Brakes Servo-assisted discs all round

Dimensions

Track	(front) 62.5in (1562.5mm) (rear) 62in (1550mm)
Wheelbase	126in (3150mm) (Pullman 153.5in/3837.5mm)
Overall length	218in (5450mm) (Pullman 246in/6150mm)
Overall width	76.8in (1920mm)
Overall height	59.5in (1487.5mm)

Once the project had been mooted and agreed, the idea behind the 600 (W100) was to build a limousine-type car to stand as a testament to Mercedes' engineering know-how. It had to be capable of meeting the motoring needs of some of the world's most important people, including heads of state.

Launched in 1963, the 600 and long-wheelbase 600 Pullman were very much in the style of their more 'sensible' saloon sisters. Largely because of their sheer size, the 600s were not pretty in the normal sense, but they unarguably had presence. To some they had a menacing look, while others saw them as typically Teutonic masterpieces that served a purpose in the most practical manner.

At just 1in (25mm) longer than the Cadillac Fleetwood Limousine, the 600 Pullman was the world's longest 'production' car, a fact that seemed to impress status-seekers. The

Above *The 600's star motif on top of the radiator grille was spring-loaded, a safety feature designed to minimize injury to pedestrians.*

Right Lichtenheiten, *huge double-bladed bumpers and bright trim over the wheel arches all added weight to one of the truly great heavyweights of the automotive world.*

standard 126in wheelbase created a car that made a huge impression on onlookers.

Body-Building Exercise

Unlike traditional cars in the 'limo' class, the 600 was of entirely modern unitary construction, immensely strong and naturally weighty. With its central, rigid passenger safety cell, and 'crumple zones' fore and aft, it arguably provided better crash protection than any of its contemporaries. Idi Amin had no fewer than eleven 600s – the car clearly suited his bulky frame!

Styling followed Stuttgart's in-house vogue, and the car, although large, was a credit to the designers. Although it was far from being pretty in the conventional sense, it could have been much worse. The large chromed radiator grille, *Lichtenheiten*, heavy bumpers, generous

Chromium-plated boot-lid badging gave a clue as to the capacity of the V8 engine up front.

Above *Ingenious wind deflector in the rear doors protected passengers from draughts, attention to detail that made a huge impression in the 1960s.*

Stainless-steel brightwork around the windows was of the highest quality, and made to last just about for ever … and a bit more.

use of brightwork and 'mid-flank' swage lines all conspired to detract the eye from the vast expanse of sheet metalwork. Designed to be imposing rather than streamlined, the 600 had the aerodynamics of a herd of sleeping pigs, but this was entirely in keeping with the lack of automotive progress being made at this end of the market. In any case, this series was largely aimed at the North American market, where streamlining was not a high priority.

Lebensraum

The dimensions of the 600's interior were intended to make passengers who lived in mansions or palaces feel at home. In standard guise, the 600 was not equipped with a lavatory, but there was little else missing from the list of features. Modern motorists take many of those features – fully reclining rear seats, hat nets, head restraints and curtains, for example – for granted, but in the 1960s they were part of an impressive and unique standard package.

Optional extras included radio and television sets, cocktail sets and a division between the passenger compartment and driver. Customers were also invited to specify odds and ends to suit their individual requirements, but no one persuaded Mercedes to 'anglicize' the upholstery or wood trim. Had they have done so the interior might have been more inviting, and less 'artificial'.

Curtains in the rear window gave privacy for passengers, and also obscured rear-view vision for the chauffeur.

For passengers the rear compartment was a place for stretching out, enjoying a drink, reading a newspaper, holding meetings, sleeping, worrying about assassination attempts – several of these cars were armour-plated – and waving to minions lining the route of a cavalcade. Despite all this, the driver's seat was the best place to be, peering through the vast windscreen along a seemingly endless bonnet. In line with Mercedes' preoccupation with safety, instrumentation was minimal, and very much in the fashion of the contemporary coupé and cabriolet range. While Jaguars, Rovers and others of the same period had a certain allure, with their rows of neat gauges sunk into polished wooden dashboards, the 600's dash was altogether more comprehensive. Bela Barenyi's view was that there should be as little as possible to distract the driver from the serious job of driving. To this end, there was a central combination gauge flanked by the speedometer and tachometer. Encased in a polished wood binnacle, purely for decorative purposes, the gauges were as aesthetically displeasing as the steering wheel and

Laundaulet versions were rare and almost exclusively used for state occasions. Despite its great length, the chassis was sufficiently rigid to cope with the loss of the rear part of the roof.

The ultimate in exclusive, high-speed travel, the 600's interior was ideal for conducting business on the move, or simply relaxing and enjoying a drink in almost complete silence.

column-mounted gear lever, but they were undeniably practical.

Central locking, power-assisted windows, hydraulically powered seats and door-mounted rear-view mirrors (manually adjustable from inside) were all novelties that impressed most observers. These widgets were more a show of Mercedes know-how than anything else – a demonstration in the use of state-of-the-art gadgetry, simply because it had been invented. Double-glazed windows, though, would have to wait for the future.

Many ordinary folks in Europe did not have a telephone or television in their house during the 1960s; the presence of these two gadgets in a car was an indication of the importance, power and wealth of its owner.

Instruments, controls and steering wheel were all in keeping with standard Mercedes thinking. The wood veneer moulding of the instrument binnacle showed that German craftsmen were every bit as skilled as their British counterparts.

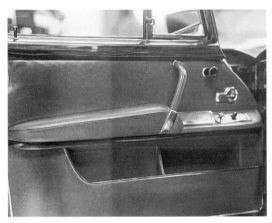

Above *Even in the short-wheelbase version, rear legroom was more than ample. Leather-covered upholstery was firm and supportive in true German tradition.*

Above left *The leather-faced door panelling had deep stowage bins, generously proportioned armrests, a cigar lighter and ashtray, and switchgear for operating the windows. Extremely heavy and large, the doors closed with the sound of a brief, muted explosion.*

Left *Rear passengers were accorded the same features on their doors, as well as a switch to adjust the seat.*

By contrast with the instrument binnacle, the wood veneer behind the windscreen looked cheap and incongruous in a car that boasted so many technically advanced features.

Typically, the power systems worked reliably for many years. The majority of these machines were always kept in tip-top 'no-expense-spared' order, which is why lengthy restoration work today, although inherently expensive, is seldom needed. Some cars did lead a hard life and were not maintained as prescribed; surely only a complete maniac would embark upon a ground-up restoration of such an example – but such people are not unknown in the world of old cars!

A Piece of Eight

From a financial viewpoint it would have suited the people in Sindelfingen to have used one of their existing 6-cylinder engines to power the big 600. In reality, any of the company's 'sixes' would have been inadequate.

The 600's 6332cc fuel-injection engine was Daimler-Benz's first production V8 to be fitted to a car. Developing 300bhp at 4,000rpm, it was capable of propelling this heavyweight to a top speed of 130mph (210km/h).

Instead, Mercedes took the most obvious route, though it would prove to be expensive, and produced a brand-new V8 to compete head-on with the best from Detroit and Britain. With a bore and stroke of 103 x 95mm, the resulting 6332cc was large by any standards. With a single overhead camshaft per bank of cylinders, fuel injection and 9:1 compression ratio (or optional 7.3:1), there was no less than 250bhp (net) at 4,000rpm, sufficient for a top speed of 130mph (210km/h), and blasts to 60mph from rest in just under 10 seconds. In terms of out-and-out performance it was capable of living with the 2-litre Porsche 911T (but not the 911S) in a straight line, but the Merc's fuel consumption was rarely better than 12mpg (23.5l/100km) – and considerably less for those who could not resist temptation with the throttle pedal.

Despite the crudity of its cast-iron cylinder block – alloy was used for the heads – this was a complex piece of engineering, with an eight-plunger fuel-injection pump resembling an engine in itself. Because of all the engine-driven pumps to run the air-conditioning, air suspension, brakes, steering and the rest, no less than 50bhp was sapped long before it had a chance of being transmitted to the tarmac. This

was equivalent to the maximum output of the twin port 1600cc Volkswagen Beetle, the most powerful of all standard Beetles produced at Wolfsburg from 1970.

Rolls-Royce was never in the habit of quoting power-output figures for its superb V8 engines – revealing such details was considered at Crewe to be the ultimate in vulgarity – but the contemporary Phantom V was capable of around 120mph (195km/h). It is doubtful that this figure was established on public roads; after all, stately limousines should always be driven with decorum and dignity. For this reason, a close-ratio five-speed 'sports' gearbox was out of the question, and all 600s were fitted with a beefed-up version of Daimler-Benz's four-speed automatic and limited-slip differential. The gear ratios were as follows; first 3.98, second 2.52, third 1.58, fourth 1.1, reverse 4.15 and final-drive 3.23.

No Air-Heads

With the equivalent weight of approximately five camels, everything about the 600's chassis was engineered to remain unnoticed by those who experienced the car's supple ride and

The low burbling noise from the tail pipes – one on each side – turned to a classic V8 growl under hard acceleration.

On the road the 600 had the performance and roadholding capabilities of some contemporary sports cars, but fuel consumption was never any better than 10mpg (28l/100km) and half this figure if the big V8 was made to work hard.

30 Abnahme

DER LETZTE
MERCEDES 600

BB-041299

Sales of the 600 – 2,677 were built all told – fell away sharply after the Middle East oil crisis of 1973, but production did continue until 1981. Many of the cars produced in the later years were purchased by oil-rich Arabs.

powerful brakes. The set-up was inherently complex, and unsung mechanics were occasionally called upon to sort out problems, particularly with the air-suspension system, which were part and parcel of the attempts to 'reinvent' the coil spring.

Up front there were conventional wishbones, dampers and anti-roll bar, but compressor-driven bags in place of steel springs. The rear was much the same, except that the suspension was self-levelling, and could also be controlled by the driver for height and occasion depending on the level of comfort required. To some misguided critics, the only flaw in the design was the low-pivot swing-axle system – at a time when the majority of

British cars continued to use cart springs, 'live' rear axles and sick bags for their poor passengers.

Braking was by power-assisted discs on all four wheels, with a dual-circuit system for reassurance in the event of one system failing. Interestingly, the 15in diameter road wheels, closed with chromed hubcaps and bright trims, were made of ordinary pressed steel throughout the 600's entire production life. This was understandable in the early days, when aluminium-alloy was not generally used for the more expensive cars. In another sense it was surprising; Daimler-Benz alloys came on stream as optional extras on the SL sports cars at the end of the 1960s, but no one thought to fit them to the 600s.

The driver of a Mercedes 600 could really look forward to a day's work. Ride quality and handling were unrivalled, and roadholding was almost faultless. Under heavy braking or cornoring, a Cadillac became rather unstable, as did the Phantom V Rolls. However, the Mercedes could genuinely be hustled in the manner of a sports car. The 600 was certainly capable of giving a Healey 3000 a run for its money, although one cannot quite imagine Eugen Böhringer gliding through the forests of mid-Wales in a rally-prepared 600, hot on the heels of Pat Moss in the hairiest of British sports cars...

But It Had to Go

The 600 was virtually handbuilt and available only to order, after a deposit had been paid, so production – finally halted as late as 1981 – was always at no more than a trickle. The cars were extremely expensive, with the Laundelet version available from 1965 being the grandest and most expensive of all. Between 1963 and the end of production, a total of 2,677 cars were built. The profit margin on each example was slender, but the 600 was a global flagship for Daimler-Benz; the company had a reputation to protect, and allowing a rival to take over the mantle of

'manufacturer of the world's finest car' was never on Stuttgart's agenda.

The company produced virtually every type of vehicle, but needed to soldier on with the 600 as much for political reasons as any others. As an elitest vehicle it exceeded every expectation, particularly appealing to heads of state who could not use a Rolls or Cadillac for fear of being accused of political bias towards Britain and America.

This would remain the case for many years, and, although modern Mercedes limousines continue as official transport for politicians and others in many countries, BMW has provided the stiffest competition in this area since the mid-1990s. Much has changed in the market since the Middle East oil crisis of 1973, after which designers and engineers were required to change direction over the gas-guzzlers they had been producing. BMW's ownership of Rolls-Royce and VW's of Bentley may have certain ramifications, but history records that the first of the modern breed of 'top-drawer boulevardiers' was produced by Daimler-Benz. For the company that invented the motor car, being second has never been good enough.

3   The Super Saloons

S-Class from 1965

With Borgward having ceased trading at the beginning of the 1960s, BMW being content at that time to cultivate the mid-range sports saloon class, and Volkswagen struggling to cope with demand for Beetles in ever-increasing

Launched in 1965, the S-Class saloons were conservatively styled by Paul Bracq, and followed BMW practice in having a large glass area for improved all-round vision. The radiator grille was as imposing as ever.

numbers, Daimler-Benz continued to increase its profits with a comprehensive range of cars with broad appeal.

Sales of Fintails exceeded initial expectations, but the board was hatching plans for a range of really upmarket cars at about the same time that the world was hovering on the brink of all-out nuclear war. The new S-Class was launched in 1965, setting new standards and prompting both BMW and Jaguar to follow suit. Many manufacturers would try to emulate the design concepts of the S-Class over the

The same model – the 280S – arguably looked better in the darker colours.

years, but only BMW would succeed in making genuine improvements.

Designer Paul Bracq was in charge of the car's styling, creating what some saw as the dullest of dullards; others viewed it as a timeless embodiment of automotive good taste and conservatism. The body was without the infamous tail-fins, which had become badly outdated, and the look of the car did not easily define its nationality. It was neither typically European, German, American nor British; this was a new Merc, and customers were invited to take it if they had sufficient money, or leave it if they had not.

Bracqish beyond doubt

By modern standards, and with the benefit of hindsight, the S-Class appears as an unremark-

able three-box saloon, with the inevitable Mercedes hallmarks of *Lichtenheiten* and a large, chromed radiator grille. In reality, the car was light years ahead of its time, and embraced the safety features established by Bela Barenyi several years previously. *The Motor* made the following remarks on this subject:

> Mercedes have been pioneers in research into car safety. On the 250SE the bumpers form a separate part of the chassis and are faced with rubber, and the door handle buttons are recessed so that they cannot release the doors in a side-swipe. The hull of the car is tremendously strong and the cabin has been proved practically uncrushable in all kinds of high-speed accidents.

Very much in keeping with the 230SL 'Pagoda', there was an enormous glass area, and correspondingly narrow roof pillars, for first-class all-round vision. Curved glass in the side win-

*A handsome, if
aesthetically unexciting
three-box saloon, the
S-Class was an ideal
family model with a
variety of powerful
6-cylinder engines with
both carburettors and
fuel injection.*

A handsome, if aesthetically unexciting three-box saloon, the S-Class was an ideal family model with a variety of powerful 6-cylinder engines with both carburettors and fuel injection.

dows increased shoulder room in both the front and rear by an appreciable margin. Small but quite ingenious details included an anti-surge reservoir for the fuel tank, a two-way adjuster for the driver's seat, and quick-release levers for the quarterlights ('borrowed' from the 600).

By comparison with the Fintails, the bonnet was lower, the upper surface of the boot lid was flatter and the tail lamps were less conspicuous. And, as *The Motor* pointed out in its 1965 road test, 'Curiously, the new body contains no extra sound deadening material – curious because

the quietness of this model compared with its predecessor is quite striking.'

Predictably, the exterior had plenty of brightwork – chrome was still very much in contemporary vogue and Merc owners were not denied it.

No-Log Cabin

The interior was entirely new, spacious and 'dangerously' comfortable – just the sort of place a weary soul could sleep, protected from the anti-capitalist protestors of the 1960s. In standard guise the cars had perforated Tex vinyl upholstery, which was hard-wearing and looked uncannily like leather. Genuine leather was available at extra cost, but it resembled vinyl (one area of car design in which British manufacturers continue to lead the Germans).

Daimler-Benz incorporated many interior safety features that the Americans would have enshrined in law by the late 1960s. They included recessed door handles, flexible rubber knobs on the window winders, burst-proof door locks, a 'snap-away' rear-view mirror and heavily padded steering-wheel boss. Where

Rear styling was similar to that of the Fintail, but without the fins; most agreed that Bracq and company had returned to their senses.

The S-Class cars had little real competition; the British largely remained loyal to Rover – punitive purchase tax on foreign imports saw to that – and the French enjoyed their superb DS Citroëns, but the Mercedes was the class act of the field.

The 250, 280 and 300 shared similar roadability and driving characteristics, but the later 6.3-litre car demonstrated just how well sorted the chassis was in the 'lesser' models.

primary and secondary safety are concerned, no one working in the car industry would argue seriously against the widely held view that, over the generations, the S-Class Merc has been the safest of all cars. Three decades after its launch, it was almost impossible to believe that Diana, Princess of Wales could have sustained fatal injuries while riding as a passenger in an S-Class.

The layout of the instruments and controls largely followed the style of the coupés and

Upper and lower surfaces of the dashboard and the central pad of the steering wheel were heavily padded for safety, in a decade that saw consumer groups, initially headed by US lawyer Ralph Nader, become a powerful force against motor manufacturers.

cabriolets, although wood was not featured on the dashboard. Mercedes had discovered that this material was inclined to fragment during serious collision and, in view of its potential for causing injury, the planners took a more modern approach.

Despite the agreeable travelling environment created, the interior was not without its critics. Some commentators, particularly in Britain, eschewed the column-mounted gear lever and 'umbrella-type' handbrake lever under the dashboard. The latter 'afflicted' the Porsche 356 and came in for stick for the same reason. *The Motor*'s testers complained that, although the heating and ventilation systems were 'good', there was a tendency on rainy days for the interior to mist up and 'took a long time to clear', adding that, 'on the test car, the heater unit was hidden behind a badly attached piece of fibre-board above the transmission tunnel, which was most out of keeping with the general air of a luxury car. Also, the carpets were not firmly fixed to the floor and rucked up easily.'

Others considered that the rear lacked sufficient legroom – such a large car was expected to offer even more – but, by and large, Mercedes had done their homework well enough for most.

Engine Designate

The four models in the S-Class range comprised the 250S, 250SE, 300SE and long-wheelbase 300SEL, making seventeen models in the Merc line-up all told. Both 250s had the existing 2.5-litre engine, the S with dual twin-choke Solex carburettors and 130bhp, and the SE with fuel injection and 150bhp. The 3-litre had the all-alloy unit developing 170bhp.

On the 250SE, revisions to the Bosch fuel-injection system included a more accurate six-plunger fuel pump in place of the twin-plunger unit, and fuel metering controlled by a mechanical linkage instead of being relayed through a diaphragm responding to the inlet manifold depression.

The car was accommodating and spacious, with comfortable seating and ample headroom, but a number of nitpickers complained of insufficient legroom.

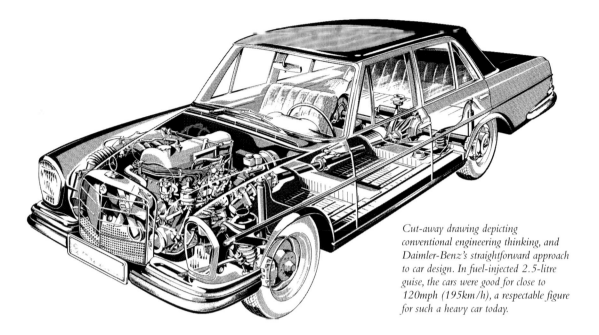

Cut-away drawing depicting conventional engineering thinking, and Daimler-Benz's straightforward approach to car design. In fuel-injected 2.5-litre guise, the cars were good for close to 120mph (195km/h), a respectable figure for such a heavy car today.

Of the 250SE *Autocar* commented that 'with its seven-main-bearing crankshaft, the engine is ultra smooth, although once above its peak power revs it makes itself heard rather than felt. With only 2.5 litres to propel a car weighing the better part of 1.5 tons, the engine has to do a lot of work, and it is designed to do just this.'

With a fair top speed of 114mph (182.5km/h), the ability to reach 60mph from rest in 10.8 seconds and 80mph in 20.4 seconds, the 250SE provided something of a benchmark in its class. *Autocar's* testers, however, could never better 17.9mpg (15.8l/100km), the car dipping to less than 14mpg

Designated as a W109 – the rest of the range was officially the W108 – the long-wheelbase version of the 300SEL was 4in (100mm) longer than the standard car. The 'L' designation, however, stood for Luftfederung *(or 'air-suspension').*

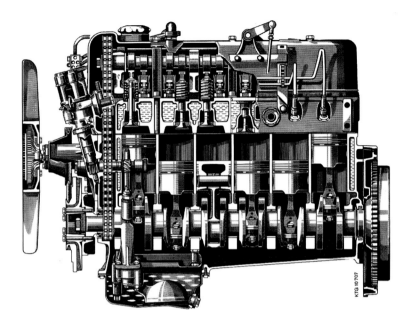

The in-line 6-cylinder engine, with its chain-driven single-overhead camshaft and seven-bearing crankshaft, was conventional for an engine of this type, but in production at a time when the majority of 'cooking' saloons utilized considerably less sophisticated units with pushrod actuation of the valves.

(20l/100km) at one juncture. As the magazine remarked, 'Treated more sedately, this car should return closer to 20mpg (14l/100km/h), but we doubt if even a chauffeur would do any better.' Such is the progress made in the past thirty years or so that a modern 2.5-litre 6-cylinder car – a BMW 525i, for example – can easily accomplish 33mpg (8.5l/100km).

The 250S by contrast was capable of 0–60mph in 12.6 seconds, and a maximum speed of 107mph (170km/h), figures which underlined the difference between carburettors and the superiority of fuel injection. Like the majority of its contemporaries, the 250S was happiest cruising at 80–90mph (125–145km/h); at this speed, it allowed for relaxed and rapid travel, notwithstanding constant noise from the Firestone Phoenix radial tyres.

Competition from Britain included the 4.2-litre Jaguar Mk10, Vanden Plas 4-litre R, Rover 3-litre and Humber Imperial. Of the group, the 250S Mercedes was the third-fastest, the safest, the best-made and by far the most expensive. In Britain, it retailed at more than £3,000 – £600 more than the Jaguar –

but this hefty sum included more than £500 of purchase tax. On the face of it, the Jaguar appeared to provide the best value, at least for those who could live with the big cat's 6ft 6in girth, huge appetite for fuel, cad's image and terminal body corrosion. At £2000 the handsome Rover 3-litre was solidly made, enjoyed a proven track record in international rallying and performed well, while the Vanden Plas and Humber were dinosaurs in the worst tradition of British ineptitude.

A Transmission of Power

Although slightly more than half the S-Class cars sold were fitted with Daimler-Benz's excellent four-speed manual synchromesh gearbox, automatics were gaining in popularity on all types of luxury cars. All four models carried the auto option, and indeed it was standard on the 300SEL.

The Daimler-Benz automatic gearbox, which used a simple fluid clutch instead of a conventional torque converter, was undoubtedly one of the best and smoothest from a

European manufacturer, but lagged some way behind American versions. Designed for use in conjunction with much larger engines, the Detroit two- and three-speed automatics were notably smoother in operation and, because of the torque produced by large-capacity power units, gear changing was always minimal.

The Mercedes gearbox could be used in fully automatic mode, but with provision for manual override if required. *The Motor* noted that 'with the lever at 4, full throttle acceleration will cause upward changing at about 29, 46 and 78mph [46.5, 73.5 and 125km/h]'. The magazine report went on to say, 'This transmission can be summed up as offering a much greater than usual degree of control for the driver with sporting instincts or for coping with adverse conditions, without much loss of refinement in the change mechanism. Some credit for this must go to the combination of low-speed torque with high peak revs, which makes it possible to use third as an effective overtaking gear well beyond the legal speed limit in Britain.'

The same writer criticized the quantity of mechanical noise from the gearbox, but considered this to be quite normal for a Mercedes, and also complained that the brake pedal was of 'single width'.

After a year in production, the 300SEL was offered with five-speed manual transmission, a sensible response to customer demand. Customers reckoned that, having been asked to pay roughly twice the price of a 250S, they ought to have the choice of a conventional stick. Daimler-Benz agreed and duly obliged.

Despite the manual option the range-toppers were almost always fitted with automatic transmission, and not everyone warmed to it. Of the later 2.8-litre 300SEL *The Motor* made the following remarks:

The gearbox is at its worst when driving all out: set at 4 (fully automatic) the intermediate maxima are not only low (barely 70mph [110km/h] in third) but uncomfortably abrupt; certainly nothing like the smooth imperceptible slur of a really good automatic. At a more sedate pace, the changes are inconspicuous enough and with practice it is possible to smooth them out even more by lifting the throttle at the right moment.

This same writer advised judicious use of the manual override, but ultimately concluded that the car was far better with the five-speed manual gearbox. Despite automatic gearboxes having been virtually perfected in recent times, some die-hards of the old school continue to be prejudiced against them, probably because of experiences with the crude versions of the 1960s. Those who considered Daimler-Benz auto gearboxes to be wanting needed only to compare them with a similarly equipped BMC Mini.

Down the Road

It goes without saying that there was all-round independent suspension – by wishbones, coil springs, additional rubber springs and telescopic dampers up front, and low-pivot swing axles, coil springs, rubber springs, compensating spring and telescopic dampers at the rear – servo-assisted disc brakes on all four wheels, and power-assisted steering by Daimler-Benz's recirculating-ball system.

So much for its mechanical parts, but the true worth of an S-Class could only be appreciated in its natural environment – being driven. To those whose perceptions of the S-Class were of a flabby sybarite with poor handling, the big Merc was a product of Germany picking itself up after the war. In reality, the car was light years ahead of everything else in the big league.

Such cars were rarely driven at the limit of tyre adhesion by their owners – they were not those kind of cars – but journalists would give it a go, and found little to moan about with the

A publicity shot from Daimler-Benz's archive in which the car stands out against the dullest of backgrounds – a sure indication of the conservative image that the company sought to portray during a decade of radical social change.

Mercedes. Ride comfort was first class, there was never excessive body roll, and the power-steering was far superior to that found on many American contemporaries.

According to *Autocar*, 'To all intents and purposes the 250SE understeers, but when taken right to the limit – and that is faster than any owner is likely to drive the car – there is sudden and violent oversteer, which corrects itself as soon as power is taken off and the steering unwound.'

By comparison *The Motor's* commented as follows:'Driven fairly fast over a familiar stretch of undulating secondary road the Mercedes proved one of the most comfortable cars we have ever driven. Owing to the self-levelling device in the rear suspension there is no reason why the ride should deteriorate even when the maximum permissable load is carried.'

Opposite *A similarly unimaginative publicity shot, showing that most powerful of symbols – the star motif – standing aloft to emphasize the prestige associated with Mercedes ownership.*

However, not everybody was over-impressed with the car's braking performance. When Bill Boddy tested the 230SL for *Motor Sport* he found the brakes on this otherwise unflawed sports-cum-GT to be 'spongey'. *The Motor*'s people were less than complimentary about the anchor power of the S-Class, pointing out an over-sensitivity to light pedal pressures, a tendency for the car to pull to one side under emergency conditions, a rise in pedal pressure after 'fade' tests and a barely adequate handbrake.

280S (W108) 1968–72	
Engine	
Cylinders	6
Bore × stroke	86.5mm × 78.8mm
Capacity	2778cc
Compression ratio	9:1
Fuel system	2 Zenith 35/40 INAT
Max power	140bhp
Max torque	165lb ft at 3,600rpm

By 1968, the price of the 250S, for example, had crept up to nearly £3500 in Britain – the equivalent of four 1500cc VW Beetles, and a hefty amount to pay for a car that was clearly not without its faults. No car of this era was entirely free from what today's classic-car journals describe as 'character', but Mercedes had plenty of scope for improvement. The jerky automatic transmission, 'interesting' brakes, and tyre noise on poor surfaces were all cause for polite, but unequivocal, press comment.

Concluding its report on the 250S, *The Motor* commented that 'there is, nevertheless, something uniquely wholesome about the intrinsic quality and appeal of a Mercedes which still commands more respect than we can proffer to most other cars'.

Naturally, the cars were developed, but there were comparatively few changes during the first couple of years of production. There was improved cabin ventilation, and cursory changes to relatively unimportant 'widgetry' were carried out, but it was typical of Daimler-Benz that the designers and engineers had completed their research sufficiently well at prototype stage not to worry about 'facelifts', and changes for the sake of fashion.

More, or Less

Although the 250S was retained until 1969, a new range was launched in 1968, comprising the 280S, 280SE, 280SEL and 300SEL. Confusingly, all four had the 2.8-litre 6-cylinder engine, which also found its way

An enduring classic and considered by some to have been the finest saloon of its day, the mighty 6.3-litre version of the 300SEL was launched to great acclaim in 1967.

into the 280SL sports car at roughly the same time.

On the face of it, this move appeared to be something of a backward step, particularly in the case of the 300s, but there was method in their madness, as always with Daimler-Benz. At entry level, the twin-carburettor 280S delivered a respectable 140bhp, while the fuel-injected 280SE and SEL developed 160bhp. At 170bhp the 300SEL was no more powerful than the outgoing 3-litre car, which was something of a credit to the engineers, as this figure had been achieved with 200cc less.

There was little performance differential between the four models, with top speeds ranging between 113mph and 120mph (181 and 195km/h). On the increasingly congested roads of Europe, this was judged by most to be more than adequate. The vast majority of the cars were made with automatic transmission, an initiative that was clearly customer-led.

All four cars were well equipped, expensive to buy and run, and superb to drive. Of the 280S, *The Motor* commented favourably upon the useful gain in torque, which increased acceleration most markedly between 20 and 50mph (35 and 80km/h). The report's writer went on to say that, 'In other respects, the 280S remains virtually the same as the 250S we tested before... a superbly engineered car, meticulously made, equipped and finished though, for its very high price, by no means lavishly furnished and trimmed. If you dislike superfluous decoration – and the elegant 280S certainly doesn't need it – then the relatively austere decor is a definite advantage.'

The same magazine also tested the 300SEL, and described it as a car for 'tycoons down to their last million'. In contrast with the 250S, the 300SEL was equipped with every conceivable luxury – only to be expected in a car costing £5625 in 1968. As *The Motor* put it, 'The rich smell of expensive cow hide and firm but shapely seats welcome you aboard. The door shuts with a single muffled donk, like that of a railway carriage in an acoustic chamber, and suddenly the outer world is

300SEL 6.3 (W109) 1967–72

Specifications as for 300SEL except for the following:

Engine	As for 600
Gearbox Ratios	Automatic
First	3.98:1
Second	2.46:1
Third	1.58:1
Fourth	1:1
Reverse	4.15:1
Final-drive	2.85:1

Offering high-speed stability, superior road manners and sheer high-speed performance, the 6.3 made for an entertaining track car. In fact, it was intended as a comfortable and safe inter-city express for those who could afford to burn fuel at the rate of 12mpg (23.5l/100km), or even less!

every inch a driver's car. Handling and road-holding were in a class of their own, braking was powerful and the power-steering was, according to *The Motor*, only bettered by that

remote and strangely silent. A clock ticks but you don't see the dial at first because it is badly masked by dinner-plate crash padding on the large black steering wheel behind which intricately coloured and calibrated dials peer at you from a raised binnacle.'

Like everyone who drove these magnificent carriages, the people at *The Motor* disliked the automatic gearbox for its 'jerkiness', but in all other respects considered it to be virtually peerless. Despite its weight and size, it was

Twin headlamps with halogen bulbs and spotlamps were fitted as standard on the 300SEL 6.3, but few external features distinguished it from its considerably less powerful sister.

The rectangular but neatly executed rump, with purposeful twin exhaust tailpipes, badged as a 6.3 on the right-hand side of the boot lid.

Chrome-plated bumpers were 'double-bladed', and extremely effective against clumsy parking, but added to the image of the car as a heavyweight.

The later optional alloy wheels were to the same pattern as those fitted to other models in the range. The high-profile radial tyres date this car to a period when some considered that tyre manufacturers were not doing enough to keep pace with increasing engine and chassis performance.

of the Wankel-engined NSU RO80. So much more than a tycoon's wheels, the 300SEL was almost, but not quite, everything that well-heeled Mercedes devotees could want.

Gorblimey Mate

During the 1960s, a number of power-crazy folk shoehorned a Jaguar engine into a BMC Mini, to create a car that would go 'like hell'. For the benefit of similar drivers who were looking for some adventure, Daimler-Benz came up with its own idea of an upper-middle class 'hotrod'.

Dubbed as the 300SEL 6.3, the car was publicly debuted at the 1968 Geneva Motor Show; onlookers shook their heads in disbelief. Everywhere they went, journalists also shook their heads. The 6.3 was an automotive apparition that defied the normal rules – the 6332cc V8 engine had been taken from the 600, and booted into the front of the 300SEL bodyshell. With a top speed of 134mph (215km/h), the potential to reach 60mph from rest in 7.1 seconds and to do the standing quarter-mile in 15.5 seconds, this was the ultimate in 1960s Grand Tourers (and would by no means disgrace itself in hallowed company today).

With air-conditioning and a radio – both were extra-cost options – the car retailed in Britain for a whacking £8,200 – slightly more than the fabulous Ferrari Daytona launched in 1968. The big Merc was extraordinary in that

Top *When there was a requirement for a big boot space, a big boot space is what Mercedes provided…*

Middle *Dashboard layout of the 6.3 invited criticism, with the feeling that a car in this class should have offered more in the way of sporting interior style. Mercedes were big enough to disagree.*

Bottom *The exquisite woodwork at the base of the windscreen on Martin Cushway's car is original, and subsequently the varnish has cracked rather nicely with age. Restoration to original condition would be almost unforgivable.*

The sumptuous leather seat covers were perforated to allow ventilation. The wood trim on the front and rear doors was a trend that, regrettably, shows no sign of abating even in the twenty-first century.

Below *The S-Class had subtle bonnet curves, a less 'box-like' shape and a large glass area.*

it was a match for almost every sports car of the day, but at the same time provided the luxury and comfort of a Rolls-Royce Silver Shadow. The Rolls, incidentally, had not a hope of competing with the 6.3 where performance or roadability were concerned.

Autocar's response was as follows:

> The car uses the American formula of a big vee-8 engine in a roomy body for maximum comfort and performance. But it betters equivalent American products in practically every respect, especially handling, brakes, safety, comfort, economy and even performance. The tremendous superiority in handling is the key to what makes the 6.3 Mercedes such an exciting vehicle, and so essentially a driver's car. The responsiveness of all its controls makes it a delight to drive.

True to form

The car's overall specification held few surprises, but it was the sum of the parts that excelled. The power unit was the 90-degree V8, with a single overhead camshaft per bank. With a compression ratio of 9:1 and Bosch fuel injection, the unit developed 250bhp at 4,000rpm and 369lb ft of torque at 2,800rpm. The engine, incidentally, was 'red-lined' at 5,250rpm.

Daimler-Benz's own four-speed automatic gearbox was mated directly to the engine, and had the following ratios: first 3.98, second 2.46, third 1.58, fourth 1:0, reverse 4.15 and final drive 2.85.

Few, including hardened journalists accustomed to driving quick machinery, could readily accept that the 6.3 was as dynamic as it proved to be. Bowling along in unruffled comfort, there was minimal mechanical noise, even under hard acceleration, as the engine's elephantine torque propelled the car, with or without five occupants, effortlessly to 120mph (195km/h) and beyond.

On the *Autobahnen* of Germany, where speed limits were gloriously absent, it was possible to drive in complete safety for hours at a

time at speeds that would have been impossible elsewhere in the world. The *Autocar* testers once covered 105 miles (almost 170km) in one hour, without undue stress to the car or its occupants. As the writer of the magazine's 1969 report commented, 'Most impressive were the lack of noise at high speed, and the feeling of security and confidence which the car imparted. Much is owed to the precision of the power-assisted steering, and to the excellent directional stability.'

In an attempt to find fault with the big Merc, *Autocar* misguidedly criticized the tendency of the Continental tyres to make a 'noise' under hard cornering on the winding roads of Austria.

Naturally, most journalists tended to compare the Mercedes with its British counterpart from Rolls-Royce. In terms of performance, however, the nearest British rival was Jensen's stylish Interceptor. Despite its faults, this American-engined V8 was widely acknowledged as a

280SE 3.5 (W108) 1971–72	
Engine	
Cylinders	V8
Bore × stroke	92mm × 65.8mm
Capacity	3499cc
Timing	Single-overhead camshaft per bank
Fuel system	Bosch electronic fuel injection
Compression ratio	9.5:1
Max power	200bhp at 5,500rpm
Max torque	211lb ft at 4,000rpm
Transmission	
Gearbox	automatic
Ratios	
First	3.98:1
Second	2.39:1
Third	1.46:1
Fourth	1:1
Reverse	5.46:1
Final-drive	3.46:1

As sophisticated and good as the 1960s S-Class undoubtedly was, its 1970s successor would quickly make the original car look very dated.

powerful sports-cum-GT express, yet the Mercedes was quicker in the standing-start quarter-mile, quicker at 0–60mph, had a higher top speed, and used less fuel (typically, 15mpg, or 19l/100km, overall for the Mercedes).

The statistic of acceleration from 50 to 70mph in just 4 seconds is almost meaningless on paper, but the reality of such performance hits home when attempting the same test in, for example, a modern mid-range family saloon. With most, including Mercs, it takes considerably longer, and usually involves a lot of listening to a flatulent exhaust note.

In terms of straight-line speed, the 300SEL lagged behind Jaguar's 4.2-litre E-Type by 16mph (25.5km/h), and behind Porsche's 2-litre 911S by 7mph (11km/h), but was on a par with both up to 60mph (100km/h). There was no shortage of large-capacity cars that could reach high speeds, but the Mercedes-Benz differed from all in that it had handling and road-holding to match. Others, traditionally, did not.

Walking on Air

As the Daimler-Benz air-suspension system was standard on the 300SEL, it remained in its almost unmodified form on the 6.3. Up front there were the usual wishbones, telescopic dampers, anti-roll bar and self-levelling air bags, and low-pivot swing axles, telescopic dampers, anti-roll bar and self-levelling air bags at the rear.

With relatively primitive, but extremely effective, anti-dive geometry, the 6.3 was as steady and assured under heavy braking as it was sitting in a garage. In its ability to soak up bumps in poor road surfaces, this heavyweight Titan was only rivalled by the Volkswagen Beetle, which, with its swing axles and firm torsion-bar springing, could be driven across a ploughed field almost as quickly as it could on a smooth *Autobahn*.

The Merc's ride was firm but extremely taut and, as the suspension could be raised at will by 2in (5cm) for extra ground clearance, it, too, could be driven across ploughed fields! A natural understeerer in the first instance, but an oversteerer at, or beyond, the limit, the 6.3 lent

83

itself to exuberant driving for anyone who could overcome the calming effects of the car's engineering demeanour. This was never easy, and in this respect the S-Class Mercs of the modern era are much the same. Burdened, perhaps, with such weight – front to rear distribution was 54.9 to 45.1 – it was rarely a good idea to get it completely out of shape. At 1733kg (3820lb), hauling the beast back on an even keel was quite a challenge.

Autocar noted that 'the only surface which occasionally caught it out was on the approach to some corners on a little-used mountain pass, where washboard corrugations produced sharp, rather violent reactions. Little difference in ride comfort was noticed when the tyres were blown up to the "over 120mph" pressures.'

Power-assisted steering was by Daimler-Benz's recirculating ball, geared to give 3.1 turns between locks and a turning circle of 40ft (12m). The steering wheel itself was getting on for 17in (425mm) in diameter – just as 'over-size' as every other component, and well suited to those members of the Mercedes-owning community whose waistlines were only a little smaller than their wallets.

Braking was taken care of by ATE servo-assisted discs – 10.74in at the front, and 10.98in, rear – and worked as well as any other contemporary set-up. The handbrake was of the 'umbrella' variety, located under the dashboard; it appealed mostly to American tastes and worked 'adequately'.

In all other respects, the cars excelled. While the 600 Series had an important role to play as stately ambassadorial conveyance, the 6.3 300SEL was viable as an everyday driving machine for those who never had to worry about the electricity bill.

End of the 'Sicksties'

More than 6,500 6.3s found owners before production was finally axed in 1972, with US legislation governing exhaust emissions killing off one of a truly great and classic car. As a demonstration of state-of-the-art automotive integrity and know-how, the car had few or no peers. Within known scientific parameters it performed almost without fault.

Those who criticized it did so from a relative viewpoint. Motoring journalists are apt to find niggling faults, mostly for the benefit of potential customers.

By the beginning of the 1970s the honeymoon of the 1960s was over, and had to be paid for. Rolls-Royce was on the brink of serious financial crisis, despite the boom in many world economies, and Japanese manufacturers had clearly set their sights on European and American markets. In the west, extravagance and exploration were replaced by thrift and restraint. The big 6.3 Mercedes had to go, but its like would be seen again.

Size Matters

As in the case of the coupés and cabriolets, the range-topping S-Class saloons were treated to V8 power from 1969, with 3.5-litre units being placed in the 300SEL, 280SE and 280SEL. The V8 route was selected for the simple reason that the North American market more or less expected this configuration in a car contesting the title of 'Best in the World'.

Ironically, the revised cars despatched to the USA were no more powerful than the traditional 6-cylinder cars. Engine-management equipment designed to cut harmful exhaust emissions strangled performance; fuel consumption was also increased, and, not for the first time, the US government legislation had shot itself in the foot.

The 280SE and 280SEL 6-cylinder cars remained in production, but neither these, nor the V8s were available in all markets. On the production front, there were few changes, but alloy wheels became extra-cost options from

1969, and there were twin, 'stacked' headlamps as on the 6.3-litre car. To a multi-spoke design, with star motifs at their centre, the alloys are still regarded as pieces of classic design.

In European spec, the 3.5-litre V8s gave good performance – close to 130mph (210km/h) was easily attainable – and although the engine was criticized by some for its high level of mechanical noise, it was extremely reliable and possessed masses of usable torque. Interestingly, Rover also swapped its trusty 'six' during the 1960s, for the Buick-designed 3.5-litre pushrod V8, but the cars fitted with this unit were not in the same league as the S-Class Mercedes.

To overcome increasingly stringent US legislation governing exhaust emissions, the 280SE, 280SEL and 300SEL were fitted with 4.5-litre V8 engines from 1971. Although able to run on unleaded fuel – not necessarily the environmental advantage often claimed – this was not a success. In US spec the cars developed the same 200bhp as their 3.5-litre counterparts, but used considerably more fuel and polluted the atmosphere with yet more carbon dioxide. The move had been forced upon Daimler-Benz by the US legislature, whose members were clearly dictating the shape of automotive things to come.

By 1972, the traditional S-Class range was dead, production halted to make way for a new breed of super saloons. There is little doubting the success of the former from 1965; nearly 400,000 were made all told, and they were largely responsible for the continuation of Daimler-Benz's global image as a prestige marque. Despite the looming oil crisis of 1973, Porsche, Volkswagen, BMW and Daimler-Benz all remained well positioned to ride the storm, caused largely by politicians.

4 'Neue Klasse'

The '200s' from 1968

As the 1960s marched on, car ownership in Europe rose inexorably upwards. Behind the scenes at Volkswagen, chief executive Heinz Nordhoff was in a state of controlled panic. The Beetle was in desperate need of replacing, apparently, but wildly increasing sales illustrat-

Launched in 1968, at the same time as BMW's mid-range 2002 saloon, the 'New Class' W114/115 range was popular from the off, and praised by journalists for its all-round ability.

ed perfectly that Nordhoff's misgivings were unfounded.

Down in Munich BMW was clearly in the ascendancy, with a broad range of sporting saloons that were also enjoying success in track competition. Only a fool would discount the threat that the 'frozen propellor' would pose. In 1968 the company launched the 2002 and 2800CS coupé; both would be hailed as classics. In the same year, the Porsche 911 would enter its fourth year of production, and become all-conquering in international rallying.

Styled in a similar way to the more expensive S-Class, the new range of 'baby' Mercs were smaller but more neatly packaged.

For its part, Daimler–Benz intentionally shied away from domestic and international competition. The spectre of Le Mans 1955 hung over the company, and for this reason it was keeping its corporate head well covered. There is no doubt that the senior Stuttgart concern would have benefited enormously from a works-backed effort in both saloon-car racing and rallying, but it was not to be. Instead, Mercedes concentrated on the expansion of its production programme, spent a fortune on advertising and marketing, and continued as *the* European manufacturer of quality saloons and 'sports' cars. Journalists continued in their efforts to

The grille and Lichtenheiten instantly identify the W114/115 as a product of Sindelfingen. Four- and six-cylinder petrol engines were available in addition to the outwardly indistinguishable diesel version.

find faults with the cars, but generally failed in their quest.

In 1968, the company launched the W115 4-cylinder and W114 6-cylinder cars, a range complementary to the existing saloons, aimed at a much broader audience. Like most cars of

Rear styling was of a utility nature to ensure that the car wouldn't date quickly. The tail lamps were also made larger to comply with US legislation.

Below *The side aspect of the car – styled by Paul Bracq and Bruno Stacco – was criticized by some for being bland, but this is how many Mercedes customers liked their cars.*

The W114/115's facia layout brought no surprises, being to the same basic design as others cars in the line-up. Like Porsches and VW Beetles from 1972, the 'New Class' were fitted with a padded four-spoke steering wheel as a concession to driver safety.

this era, the new range had been five years in the planning, and it was no coincidence that their appearance aped that of the S-Class.

Bracq with Brakes On

The new cars were designed by Frenchman Paul Bracq, whose conservative approach was in keeping with Stuttgart's in-house style. As the Lamborghini Miura had been launched a year previously, and Ferrari had followed twelve months later with the breathtaking Daytona 365GTB and Dino 246, the new Mercedes saloons were entirely ignored by teenage boys. Whatever these cars were in terms of styling, they were not glamorous, but

Below *Although the body was smaller in all directions than that of the Fintail, interior space was much improved, offering almost as much cabin room as the S-Class.*

The diesel version found favour with taxi drivers, partly because of its low operating costs and low depreciation. Global success led to healthy profits for Daimler-Benz.

they catered perfectly for people who sought 'budget' Mercedes ownership.

A three-box saloon, built according to Daimler-Benz's normal principles of a rigid central cell, and deformable 'crumple' zones fore and aft, the revised cars' external dimensions were all more modest than those of the Fintails, but not at the expense of cockpit space.

To some, the car had the word 'Taxi' writ-

ten all over its bodywork – indeed, there was no denying its wholly practical demeanour. To others it was a Mercedes-Benz, and that was all that mattered.

At the front the traditional Mercedes radiator grille was built as an integral part of the fluted and rear-hinged bonnet. *Lichtenheiten* were used on all European-spec cars, while the appearance of US-spec cars, with their traditional circular headlamps, was either improved, or ruined, according to personal taste. In US trim, the 280SL sports car also had circular headlamps, but seemed none the worse for this treatment. Inevitably, the bumpers were large, heavy, chromed and given additional protection with rubber inserts – a reflection on driving conditions, or driving standards, in increasingly congested urban areas.

The flanks were dull beyond forgiveness, the largely shapeless tracts of monotonous sheet metal broken by a protective, and decorative, rubbing strip stretching from front to rear. Undistinguished tail lamps were rectangular. However, despite the impression at first glance that Bracq had had a sleepy spell, the car's overall aesthetics were pleasing. Gently sloping 'A'

The 'stretched' long-wheelbase version was not a limousine in the true sense, but a useful people carrier.

The long-wheelbase version was also intended for taxi work.

and 'C' roof pillars, tapered upper surfaces of the front and rear wings, and distinguished bonnet fluting forced those who criticized the car for being dull to look again and think twice.

In standard form, the cars were fitted with pressed-steel wheels – alloys were available at extra cost from 1969 – closed with large hubcaps of typically Germanic appearance. In body colour with star motifs at their centre, each hubcap was as solid as a riot shield. To

begin with, crossply tyres were standard wear. Radials were extra-cost options, but became standard from 1969 and made an appreciable difference to roadholding and handling.

In Sighed the Rest

The cabin's interior was an extraordinary piece of design, boasting a whole host of safety features, as well as being a model of space utilization. It was not noted, however, for its outstanding beauty. Virtually all the surfaces

Behind the scenes in the late 1960s Daimler-Benz was developing the exciting C111 Wankel-engined cars, which, with development, would go on to record-breaking runs.

with which a high-speed human could come into contact in the event of a collision were padded, to minimize impact injury. All the switchgear was in soft plastic materials, there was the ubiquitous rear-view mirror designed to snap harmlessly away in collisons, and, of course, wood veneer was to be found absolutely nowhere on US-spec models. Europeans did not relish the prospect of being splintered by wood in the event of a crash any more than anyone else, but demanded its presence in the interior just the same.

As with previous models, instrumentation was intentionally minimal, crystal clear and dull-looking. As usual, the steering wheel was of truck dimensions, but superb to use, and the gear lever was mounted on the steering column. Customers who refused to accept this horrible device – and there were many in Britain – could make a nuisance of themselves

Improved suspension and wider, radial tyres transformed the feel of the cars, but they were far from sporting in the BMW sense; by 1968, the people in Munich had given notice of a threat to the dominance of the three-pointed star.

Opposite *The two-door coupé version joined the range at the end of 1968, and had a roofline 2in (50mm) lower than on the four-door saloon.*

by ordering a conventional floor change. The uninspiring dashboard was characterless, but the facia was at least functional, even though a radio remained an extra-cost option.

Daimler-Benz also preferred to relieve customers of additional funds for power-steering, electrically operated windows, automatic transmission, seat belts, sunroof and a heated rear window, all of which served perfectly as a means of putting Vauxhall Viva owners in their place.

The seats were to Daimler-Benz's usual high standards. A cross between a throne, a commode and a sitting-room sofa, they gave a level of comfort that was virtually unrivalled, except for those who preferred the Citroën idea of upholstery. As a bonus, the cabin gave generous space in which front and rear passengers could stretch out in all directions. A small clutch of commentators

groaned about a lack of rear legroom, but without good reason.

With its large window panes, the cabin was bright and airy, a feature of the car that in many

Conservative, yet elegant, styling would remain as a Mercedes policy until the late 1990s, and reflected perfectly the kind of people attracted to the Stuttgart carmaker's products.

ways reflected the era in which it was built. Thanks to modifications to the suspension mountings – aimed at reducing mechanical noise filtering through to the cabin – the new cars were comparatively quiet and made for refined transport.

Pillarless doors and broad 'C' pillars, fully retractable rear side windows (electrically powered at extra cost), and chromed roof rails that also doubled as attachment points for a roof rack, distinguished the coupé from the standard four-door 'tin-tops'.

and a 250 with 2.5-litre 6-cylinder petrol. A 2.8-litre 280 appeared from 1971.

Naturally, the diesel-engined cars were aimed squarely at taxi firms, but increasingly found favour with private buyers who prioritized fuel consumption over performance. With just 55bhp the 2-litre car was capable of a top speed of around 95mph (152km/h), with a tailing wind, while the 2.5-litre petrol-engined variant could accomplish 110mph (175km/h), or a whisker less in automatic guise.

In terms of out-and-out performance these Mercedes were, more or less, on a par with contemporaries from Volvo and Saab. The two Swedish manufacturers made interesting, solid,

Number Lottery

Engine variants dictated model designation of the revised cars, which were badged in a similar way to the outgoing Fintails. By and large, the engines remained unaltered from the previous range. The new models comprised 200D with the 2-litre diesel, 220 2.2-litre 4-cylinder petrol, 4-cylinder 2.2-litre 220D, 2.3-litre 4-cylinder petrol 230, 2.3-litre 6-cylinder 230

Below left *Daimler-Benz stuck to the old-fashioned 'clap-hands' windscreen wipers, simply because they worked well.*

Below right *The standard steel wheels were enclosed with one-piece hubcaps and trims – chromed and colour-keyed to the bodywork. Double-bladed bumpers with rubber inserts were used at the front.*

reliable, high-quality cars, but the Mercs always gave a little more. Speed merchants favoured the 2002 BMW, and Stuttgart really had no answer to this masterpiece from Munich.

As previously, four-speed manual gearboxes were standard, but with revised ratios for more relaxed cruising, and a new automatic transmission as an option. This revised unit sought to address criticism of the old automatic's clumsy, notchy shifting, but not everyone considered it to be genuinely improved. American manufacturers continued to hold the upper hand with auto transmissions.

Swinging Axles Out with Swinging Sixties

Like the Volkswagen Beetle and the Porsche 356, Daimler-Benz's products – including its highly successful racing cars – had utilized swing-axle rear suspension for ages. The system worked exceptionally well, but was finally laid to rest with the W114 and W115 models. Persistent criticism that swing axles were 'dangerous' (usually from those who did not know enough about the subject) persuaded the engineers in Stuttgart that there was room for improvement.

This was also an opportunity to makes changes at the front, where 'A' arms, coil springs, gas-filled dampers and an anti-roll bar all conspired to improve ride, control (particularly under heavy braking) and roadholding. At the rear there were coil springs and a new trailing-arm system, which, in principle, was

Top *A large single wrap-around bumper was fitted at the rear of the car.*

Middle *The front part of the cabin was identical to that of the four-door saloon, but the lower roofline gave a feeling of sporting prowess and 'snugness'.*

Bottom *It was not a work of art, but the safety-inspired steering wheel was aimed at minimizing chest injuries in the event of a collision. As absurdly large as ever, the wheel was none the less pleasant in use.*

not too disimilar to the layout used by BMW for its saloon range.

In normal driving conditions, the new system made little difference to the feel of the car on the road. It was still an initial understeerer but displayed less tendency to oversteer at the limit of tyre adhesion. The tendency for 'snap-out' oversteer to occur had disappeared, the chassis becoming 'safe' for those who had failed to master the art and fun of 'opposite lock' with previous models.

With its old-fashioned recirculating-ball steering, directional precision was perfectly adequate, but far from the positive feeling gained with cars using more modern rack-and-pinion systems. Like the Volkswagen Beetle at the same time, the Mercedes also had a shear bolt in the steering column, designed to snap in the event of a collision. The idea behind this was simply to ensure that the steering wheel and column moved forwards, towards the dashboard, to minimize the possibility of serious chest injuries to the driver. Seat belts remained as extra-cost options during a period in which few took these safety-related items seriously as a means of reducing risks in accidents.

Discs brakes were used all round as standard, and increased in size, along with the move from 13-in to 14-in diameter road wheels. A 'limiter' valve was also introduced into the braking system to minimize the tendency of the rear wheels to lock up. Volvo fitted a similar device to its 140 Series cars at roughly the same time, and many others followed suit. The valve worked in a similar, but much more

Covered in soft vinyl, the centre console was comprehensively equipped with a radio and smoker's companion, and the switchgear was easily at hand, but both were aesthetically unexciting.

96

Above *With styling influenced by Detroit, the Fintail W110/111/112 range arrived in the late 1950s, the 6-cylinder cars preceding the 'cooking' 4-cylinder variants. The launch reflected growing affluence, particularly in Europe.*

The 6-cylinder cars were successful in international rallying, despite their weight and size. Belonging to Mercedes enthusiast Martin Cushway, this 220 regularly competes in modern historic events.

Above *The angular lines of the Fintail radically departed from the rounded curves of the previous Pontons; fins were fashionable and, like all fashions, they departed almost as quickly as they had arrived.*

Right *Single circular headlamps distinguished the 4-cylinder Fintails, which were also shorter in length.*

Below *A period shot from Daimler-Benz's archive depicting an association with an archetypal middle-class machine in an appropriate setting. The spectre of war had finally gone.*

Above *A perfect setting for a 6-cylinder Fintail in black.*

Dual-tone colour schemes were popular for the two-door cabriolets and coupes.

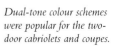

Although based on the Fintail slaoons, the cabriolet's fins were discreetly 'flattened', in the interests of good taste.

Above left *The cabriolet's imposing grille, heavy double-bladed bumpers and 'stacked' headlamps (or Lichtenheiten) were all from the traditional mould, despite the dawning of the decade of change.*

Above right *Top-quality materials, elegant design, comfort and almost unrivalled refinement led to the creation of a Grand Touring car par excellence.*

Left *Mercedes facias were frequently criticized for being bland and unexciting, especially in comparison with their British counterparts, but this is how Mercedes owners like things.*

Below *The perfect holiday destination for a cabriolet owner.*

Above *Steering wheels were always overly large, but the much-criticized instrumentation was crystal-clear and easy to read. Wood veneer on top models varied in quality.*

Above *Introduced in 1965, the conservatively styled S-Class signalled an end to the company's brief love affair with American styling touches.*

Left *An alternative to the Rolls-Royce Phantom V, the Laundaulet version of the 600 was intended for state occasions.*

Right *The world's most technically advanced limousine, the 600 was launched in 1963 and crammed with state-of-the-art gadgetry. With its 6.3-litre V8 engine and a top speed of 130mph (210km/h), it was also capable of outgunning many contemporary sports cars.*

The first S-Class cars combined luxury and comfort with performance and safety, but they were far from cheap to buy and run

Jaguar provided healthy competition for the S-Class, but the British cars, although good-looking, were not as reliable as they could be, and tended to rust.

Below *The W114 two-door coupe version, illustrated in 280CE form, looked more sporting with its roofline lowered by 2in (50mm).*

Below *Publicly unveiled in 1968, the W114/115 saloons closely resembled the luxury S-Class, and sold in huge numbers.*

Above *Fabulous mid-engined C111 research prototypes were developed in the late 1960s and 1970s as test-beds, Daimler-Benz setting up new records with diesel-engined variants.*

Left *One of the experimental sports cars is dwarfed by the W116 S-Class, but they share many of the same technical features.*

Below *Many Mercedes owners wish Daimler-Benz had put the C111 into production, for it was one of the best-looking sports cars of the 1970s.*

A classic among the 'baby' Mercs, the W123 was one of the most popular of all the saloons from Sindelfingen.

Below The W116 S-Class, a performance luxury saloon launched in 1972, set new standards in safety. Its natural rival – Jaguar's XJ6 – was not really in the same street.

Below Beyond the 1970s, the products of Daimler-Benz got better and better; this 1980s S-Class remains among the world's finest cars.

Above The utility estate version of the W123 was as versatile as the evergreen Volvo, but had greater prestige.

Upholstery was in Daimler-Benz's very high-quality Tex, an incredibly hard-wearing vinyl material.

primitive, way to modern ABS systems, and undoubtedly contributed to the overall safety of these cars.

The Merc's 'handbrake', incidentally, was a foot-operated affair on the floor, working on separate drums cast into the rear hubs. European customers gave thanks that it worked well enough but, unlike American clients, would have preferred a conventional unit operated by hand.

Far from Ended

These Mercedes saloons represented everything a well-made, top-notch family conveyance should have been. Admired by the prosperous middle classes, loathed by resentful teenagers and ignored by peroxided partygoers of this fashion-and-fad conscious age, the W114/115 Series cars were the 'sensible

The front seatbacks tipped forward at a steep angle to allow easy access to the rear seats, but people still complained about the difficulties of contorting their bodies into the required shape.

Above *With the later 2.8-litre twin-cam engine, these cars would pick up their feet under hard acceleration, causing a squatting rear end.*

Developing 185bhp at 6,000rpm with Bosch fuel injection, the 2.8-litre twin-cam engine was relatively under-stressed and offered good reliability, as well as performance.

shoes' of the motoring world. They were neither chic, outrageous, quirky nor smart, but they were made by Mercedes, which meant that they would last well in an age of growing inbuilt obsolescence, and would not go out of fashion before their time. They would also keep their residual value well.

A Cutting Plan

In addition to the regular four-door range, Daimler–Benz also introduced a most attractive two-door variant based on the W114 bodyshell. BMW was on the brink of launching its Baur-bodied cabriolet, and although the Stuttgart outfit would not take the fresh-air route, the handsome new coupé would provide a stylish alternative.

With its wide, pillarless doors and steeply angled 'C' pillars, the coupé was handsome wthout being pretty, and guaranteed to appeal to both European and American taste. The roofline was lower than the saloon's by 2in (50mm), and gave the car a more sporting, elegant look and, as on the 280SL, the roof panel was in the 'pagoda' style. The shape of the roof panel – developed by Bela Barenyi many years previously – was unique to Daimler-Benz and dictated as much by safety considerations as styling. Its origins lay in the design of the 230SL sports car, debuted in 1963. With its deep side windows and large glass area, the 230SL would have looked top-heavy with a

With a top speed of 125mph (200km/h) and the potential to accelerate from 0–60mph in just under 9 seconds, these cars were a match for the 3.5-litre V8 version of the MGB.

traditional 'flat' roof. The two outer 'humps' of the roof were, therefore, retained, while the centre part was lowered; the resulting form was not only unique and visually interesting, but immensely and inherently strong. On the new coupé, the roof also had two chrome strips from front to rear concealing mounting points for a roofrack.

One rather unnecessary 'safety feature' was a buzzer that was activated by opening a door while the key was in the ignition switch.

In addition to pillarless doors, the rear side windows were similarly pillarless – BMW adopted the same styling feature for the 2000CS coupé in 1965 and later 6-cylinder coupés from 1968 – and retracted completely into the quarter panel. There was nothing new in this; many pre-war cabriolets had the same arrangement, but it was interesting that this style of window was given a new lease of life at this time.

In the early 1960s, Ford launched its Classic coupé, with two doors and 'mid-Atlantic' styling. Aesthetically, it was less than appealing,

and it had terrible roadholding capabilities, but the truly daft thing about it was the lack of rear headroom. It was a coupé with the rear window sloping the 'wrong way', and the rear passenger quarters were cramped and uncomfortable. The Mercedes, by contrast, was spacious and comfortable because, anticipating problems well in advance, the designers had lowered the rear seat. As the backrests of the front seats were fully adjustable for rake, access to the rear seats was unimpeded.

Six-pot Power

All models of the coupé produced between 1968 and 1972 were fitted with the 6-cylinder engines common to other models in Daimler-Benz's growing range. At 'entry level', the 2.5-litre 250C developed 130bhp at 5,000rpm on twin carburettors, whereas the more expensive fuel-injected 250CE pushed out 150bhp at 5,500rpm. In regular European spec the latter ran with a compression ratio of 9.5:1, while the American, and some other markets, were served by an engine with a 7.7:1 compression ratio and just 130bhp.

By the summer of 1969 Mercedes had had to make some changes. Exhaust emissions regulations in the USA led to the 130bhp 2.8-litre engine being placed in the 250C. Some markets got fuel-injected cars, while others had carburettor versions. From 1972 to 1976, there was also a 280CE with 145bhp and fuel injection. Ironically, the US regulations concerning car safety and exhaust pollution deeply affected European car makers, while all along it was North American manufacturers that were producing the cars that contributed most to air pollution.

(Interestingly, while the majority of European manufacturers devised relatively complex means of reducing exhaust emissions, including all sorts of power-sapping 'appendages', BMW 'simply' designed an ingenious cylinder head.)

Opposite Production of the highly successful W114/115 series ended in December 1976 after more than 1.8 million units had been sold. Its successor would be even better.

By 1972, however, Daimler-Benz had been forced, again by increasingly draconian US laws, to think again. As a stop-gap the 2.8-litre engine had been ideal, but it was clearly incapable of meeting revised US demands for cleaner exhausts, while at the same time producing sufficient power.

The revised unit, also a 2.8-litre, but with a capacity of 2746cc against the outgoing unit's 2778cc, had double overhead camshafts driven from the crankshaft by a Duplex chain. A superbly smooth-running engine, it shared no components with the old 2.8-litre, and had hemispherical combustion chambers for the purpose of burning fuel more efficiently. In European format this fuel-injected engine developed 185bhp, allowing for a top speed nudging 125mph (200km/h). The cars exported to the USA were 'treated' to a single-carburetted 130bhp version, which, by comparison, felt as flat as a Ford Cortina incapacitated by several army tanks. US-spec models were also fitted with wildly extended bumpers, which did nothing to improve their appearance.

All in Good Time

By 1972, the 2.5-litre engine disappeared from production, Rolls-Royce was in crisis, Volkswagen Beetle production had peaked, BMW launched the 5 Series against the tragic background of the Munich Olympic Games, and British Leyland flogged pointlessly onwards. Around the corner of the early 1970s was yet another oil crisis, orchestrated in the Middle East and, most significantly for car enthusiasts, the English journal *Classic Cars* was launched, in 1974.

A growing band of car folk began to look to the past for motoring inspiration, showing

less and less interest in cars of the present. Modern cars tended to be dull, and, in the case of several British- and Italian-made examples, were also unreliable, badly constructed and prone to premature corrosion. Within a very short period, many older cars, particularly from the 1950s and 60s, most of which had been ignored hitherto, were suddenly hailed as 'classics'. (Of course, several were nothing of the kind, but nostalgia had begun to take over.)

Some producers, including Mercedes and BMW, continued to produce cars that got better and better, and their sales increased significantly. However, within ten years or so of the beginnings of the classic car movement, the 'mainstream' automotive industry was clearly being hit hard. A global industry specializing in the restoration of old cars began to thrive, with people spending huge quantities of money on hobby cars, rather than on new cars. The values of all 'classics' – genuine and fakes – rose artificially, until a point in the late 1980s, when huge sums were being paid often for quite undistinguished machinery. During the 1990s the editor of a once-respected English car journal even attempted to bestow classic status upon the Ford Fiesta, an idea that was greeted with hoots of laughter. In some quarters there were attempts to 'cash in' on the new industry as an investment opportunity, but the true classics remained intact and untouched by the hype and fads.

Daimler–Benz's cars of the 1960s were among the very best of their kind. Not all were classics – far from it – and few observers recognized the ones that were genuine classics as such during their heyday. Many Mercedes-Benz saloons were good workhorses, which, seemingly, went on for ever, and there have been many recent attempts to recapture motoring memories of the 1960s. Daimler-Benz's 'Oldtimer' department gives plenty of help with parts for restoration, and expert guidance.

Most restoration examples, or pristine originals, are kept for high days and holidays, or for parading at shows. A minority, especially on the African continent, continue to be hammered as everyday transport, often with bald tyres, completely spent suspension dampers and doors loosely attached to the bodywork with bits of wire.

Many of the classic Mercedes saloons of the 1960s – a 'golden' period for some – regularly change hands for a comparatively modest sum, despite superb build quality, the finest engineering integrity, and competition history. And even the sports cars – from the Gullwings of the 1950s to the 280SLs of the early 1970s – do not command the same prices as exotica from Italy. The exclusive and desirable 300SL Gullwing coupé was the most technically advanced and fastest of all the 1950s 'production' sports cars, and arguably the best-looking, but it trails a very long way in value today behind contemporaries from, for example, Ferrari. Chapter 9 explains in detail the business of buying and restoring a classic Mercedes today.

5   The 1970s

A Faster Pace

Driving on the continent in the early 1970s, particularly on the packed motorways of France, provided a great opportunity to see examples of the thousands of 'new age' cars that had begun to emerge from European manufacturers. A small number made a lasting impression and became classics overnight. Sightings might include Citroen's V6 Maserati-engined SM and the aerodynamically efficient, 'bread-and-butter' CX, Renault's beautiful Alpine A110 sports machine, hundreds of 6-cylinder BMW saloons and coupés, and of course, the new breed of technologically advanced cars from Daimler-Benz. Of these, the S-Class was among the most impressive of all road cars. As a fast, comfortable Grand Tourer, it was almost, but not quite, unrivalled. The engineers in Munich had clearly given notice, most clearly to Mercedes, that there was a German alternative to the three-pointed star.

By the early 1970s, car makers had widely adopted metallic paintwork – something of a novelty at the time – and charged extra for this seemingly desirable option. As the gleaming paintwork of these new cars glinted in the bright European sunshine, and their exhausts growled purposefully, the scene on those roads was one of motoring glamour.

Taking Stock

Few working for Daimler-Benz, or for any other German car manufacturing company,

bothered to look back to the 1960s. There was no point; the time had come to move on. Some social commentators regarded the 1960s as the decade that changed the course of the twentieth century for ever. The 1970s, it was claimed, were dull by comparison, a decade of sobriety, cultural stagnation, and questionable taste, and a period in which accountants would come to the fore.

US lawyer Ralph Nader made his own personal impact on the way in which cars were designed during the late 1960s, harping on issues relating to safety. (In fact, many of his proposals were way behind the work already done by Daimler-Benz and Porsche.) There was an upsurge in environmentalism, with 'Greens' voicing their opposition to the 'filthy' motor car. By the mid-1970s, the Red Brigade in Italy and the Baader-Meinhoff gangs, made up of the anti-capitalist educated sons and daughters of affluent middle-class families, were causing mayhem throughout Europe, with their own particular brand of violence and kidnapping. Both the environmental lobby and the terrorist gangs had a direct effect upon the motor industry, and especially upon companies producing expensive cars such as Mercedes.

On the one hand, engineers were forced to make cars more fuel-efficient, with less harmful exhaust emissions. On the other, the backlash against capitalism resulted, temporarily, in the wholesale disappearance of exotic, expensive cars from the roads of Europe. The brightly coloured paintwork of the early 1970s gave way to more sober colours; it was no longer acceptable to flaunt wealth. Bright orange, yellow and purple were replaced by grey, black and the dullest of metallic blues. Bright red Ferraris stayed in the garage, and a much more dreary alternative was used for transport to and from the office and the shops.

In the 1970s, restraint tended to be exercised throughout all levels of society. Economically, it was a difficult decade, particularly in motor manufacturing. There were new challenges – as always – and many motor manufacturers were lucky to survive. In Europe, competition, especially from the Japanese, could not be ignored. Industrial disputes in Britain and mainland Europe became

The S-Class of the 1970s was technically ahead of safety and exhaust emissions legislation originally inspired by consumer groups in the US. Although a pillar of good taste, the S-Class was symbolic of a decade in which 'restraint' in the motor industry replaced the 'excesses' of the 1960s.

everyday affairs, and even Germany was not immune to disruption. Whatever the rights and wrongs of the situation, the financial losses were significant.

Despite the difficulties, however, the big German companies became ever more successful. In part, this was due to prudent housekeeping, the production of better, much improved cars and advances in technology as a direct result of huge investment in research and development. More important, though, was the large increase in demand for cars. People throughout the west had, despite economic gloom and doom from time to time, become more prosperous. Greater access to financial credit mobilized the masses. 'Everyone' wanted a car, and 'everyone' could have one.

The scale ranged from Golfs and Polos from Volkswagen, via sporting saloons in the mid-range (and above) from BMW, to luxury cruisers from Daimler-Benz at the other. Each of the companies expanded rapidly, increasing

its range of cars and launching itself into aggressive marketing campaigns. Daimler-Benz's main plant at Sindelfingen, near Stuttgart, with its 'roofed' area of at least 500 acres, struggled to keep pace with demand. Car production was, therefore, expanded at the Bremen factory.

Porsche forged its own unique path; the Zuffenhausen company's successful programme in international sports-car racing was bringing big returns. Porsche also expanded its range, from 1975, but its new breed of front-engined cars did not meet with universal approval within the company. By the mid-1990s, Ferry Porsche's misgivings had been proved to be well-founded. Porsche's clientele wanted rear-engined sports cars, and ones with power units preferably cooled by fresh air.

Because of the rise in cost of developing new models, there was increasing co-operation between companies. Unofficially, rival designers were beginning to share their ideas, and computers began to play an increasingly important role in design studios.

Along with every other German car maker, Daimler-Benz comprehensively missed the boat in one particular area – the four-wheel-drive market. The impact made by the Spen King-designed Range Rover, launched in Britain in 1969, was relatively insignificant at first. However, the situation would change rapidly after the debut of a number of Japanese all-wheel-drive vehicles. Although the majority of customers attracted to these cars would never drive them on mud or grass, demand for 'chunky' 4x4s was destined to spiral upwards. Ferry Porsche was one of the few experts in Germany who saw future potential in four-wheel-drive, but internal politics at Volkswagen, with whom Porsche has always maintained close links, meant that his views were simply ignored.

In one respect, Daimler-Benz came to the end of an era in 1972 with the retirement of chief development engineer Rudi Uhlen-haut. An engineering genius, Uhlenhaut had worked tirelessly for the company, his illustrious career spanning many decades, including the glorious Grand Prix days of the 1930s. His successors, along with the rest of the team, would have the unenviable task of working through the aftermath of the 1973 oil crisis, and having to adapt to legislation from North America, which continued to be the company's most important and lucrative export market.

Fuel consumption had become the sudden issue of the day. Apart from building cars with more aerodynamically efficient bodies, and less weight, Mercedes stepped up production of its diesel-engined cars. For years, 'oil-burners' had been the unglamorous staple of German taxi drivers. Noisy, smelly and lacking in performance, they had a slight advantage in fuel economy over their petrol-engined counterparts. With development, though, diesels became considerably more economical and, although they were unrefined by comparison with today's offerings, the 'rediscovery' of turbocharging (by BMW) also led to diesels with good performance.

Diesels provided a quick solution to a pressing problem, and nothing has happened in the ensuing years to diminish their popularity, despite evidence that diesel particulates are damaging to human health. Through the years, the rules governing exhaust emissions have been tightened in both Europe and the USA. By the early 1990s, catalytic converters were compulsory on petrol-engined cars, and unleaded petrol was introduced as the norm. Unleaded petrol contains benzine – a known carcinogen – and catalytic converters simply do not work until an engine is operating at optimum temperature, but these facts seem to have eluded the attention of politicians and environmental lobbyists.

Engineers and designers proved to be especially adept at overcoming the challenges of the new decade. Beyond the debate over exhaust emissions, the USA also introduced the heavy burden of compulsory crash testing, and inevitably the cost of car production began to go through the roof. Many within the industry questioned the wisdom of sending a car, fitted with cameras, 'dummies' and electronic measuring gear, head on into a concrete block at 30mph. As the vast majority of road accidents do not happen in this way, and the results of such catastrophic testing were rather inevitable, it all seemed pointless.

Several companies cobbled together a number of odd creations, usually under the loosely defined heading of 'concept safety car'; in Daimler-Benz's case, they were 'Experimental Safety Vehicles' (ESF). These heavyweights, often clad in deformable rubber sections, and resembling fairground 'dodgem' cars, were demonstrably safer under crash-test conditions, but not by much. The slender margin could not, ultimately, justify the extra expense that production versions would have entailed. Their additional weight also largely negated the benefits of more fuel-efficient engines.

Daimler-Benz showed one prototype after another, each more ugly than the last. With designs tailored to protect occupants in head-on collisions of up to 50mph (80km/h), and side impacts of up to 15mph (25km/h), the company proved the point that cars could be built with a greater degree of primary safety, but with too many unrealistic compromises.

The simple fact remained that Mercedes made the world's safest production cars (although Porsche and BMW do make cars to the same high standards). In the event of a serious accident, safety experts throughout the industry would prefer to be in just one make of car – a Mercedes-Benz.

Regrettably, one hangover from the considerations about car safety in the 1970s was a crop of cars with so-called 'safety bumpers'. Designed to de-form and re-form in collisions of up to 5mph (8km/h), they actually served little purpose, other than protecting the bodywork in parking accidents. Mercedes had traditionally produced saloons in the post-war period with overly large bumpers, so the 'rubberized' monstrosities of the 1970s, projected fore and aft on deformable 'prongs', had a less alarming effect than similar items fitted to contemporary Volvos, the MGB and Triumph TR7. Even the otherwise elegant Rolls-Royce Silver Shadow lost its dignity when fitted with these horrors.

While Daimler-Benz beavered away behind the scenes developing safety-related equipment, including anti-lock braking and airbags, BMW leapt into the limelight. The Munich company, like Porsche, had long since capitalized on the benefit of running a competitions department. Until the 1973 oil crisis, the CS coupés had dominated the European Touring Car Championships, and continued on their winning way in the hands of privateers thereafter.

The later appearance of BMW's M1 supercar, and its turbocharged 4-cylinder engine that powered Nelson Piquet to victory in the 1983 Formula One Championship, saw projected BMW into the German super league. The members of the Daimler-Benz board were well aware of the fact that BMW also had a superb range of road cars, and that the car-buying public wanted them in ever increasing numbers.

Involvement in motor sport during the 1970s held the key to expansion in markets on both sides of the Atlantic for BMW, while in one sense Daimler-Benz relied on selling its cars on merit. The senior Stuttgart company's motor-sport activities were confined to works efforts with the 450SLC in international rallying. There were successes, but, then as now, the idea of a luxury GT in this branch of sport failed to send the correct signals to potential customers. Mercedes cars were perceived as elitist and, although plans were made in secrecy to expand in this area, they came to nothing; rallying was not the way forward. As the late Bill Bengry discovered, at enormous cost, luxury motor cars and rallying do not go well together. The Rolls-Royce Silver Shadow in which he competed on the 1970 London to Mexico Rally was just about the most unsuitable car he ever used on the rough and tumble of unmade roads.

Snapping at the heels of both Mercedes and BMW in the 1970s was the growing Audi concern (part of the 1930s Auto-Union company), based at Ingolstadt. With Dr Ferdinand Piëch at the helm (the man responsible for the design of many of Porsche's successful sports racing cars from 1966), this pre-war concern was destined to come to the fore through international rallying from 1980. Few could have foreseen in the 1970s that Audi would go on to build real alternatives to Mercs and BMWs by the

mid-1990s. Its range began as dependable, reliable and solid, but uninspiring and, in Germany, suffered from a rather down-market image. Huge success in international rallying from 1980 onwards with the Quattro project brought Audi massive global publicity. Ferdinand Piëch had learnt from his uncle, Ferry Porsche, that a collection of sporting accolades was the cheapest way in which any car manufacturer could bring its road-going products to the attention of the public. It is a well-known that the Joe Public loves to own a car that is closely identified with sporting success.

As far as could be determined, Daimler-Benz had not lost out in showroom sales as a

Greater access to financial credit in the 1970s gave 'everyone' the opportunity to own a car. Daimler-Benz catered for both ends of the market, but the company's non-participation in motor sport was, arguably, a big drawback.

result of the company's almost total lack of involvement in motor sport, but BMW had certainly gained massively as a result of its heavy investment in competition.

Mercedes had cultivated something of a conservative image for many years. To some, the styling of the saloon ranges since the 1950s was undistinguished, bland and dull. Daimler-Benz's board considered that the majority of the company's customers were prepared to pay for top quality, as long as the packagaing was in no way ostentatious. Even the Mercedes sports cars, which had put on vast quantities of weight over the years, could no longer honestly claim to be 'Super Light', as their SL badging proclaimed. These cars were, however, absolutely correct for the sort of people who were attracted to the marque.

Daimler-Benz was beginning to forget about its great sporting past, seemingly oblivious to the huge detriment that this would bring. By the time Mercedes woke up to this inescapable fact, the company had a lot of catching up to do, but it did not take long.

Into the 1980s and Beyond

Devotees of international sports-car racing were, by and large, glad to see the end of the 1970s. After exciting prototypes such as the Porsche 917 and Ferrari 512S had, in effect, been banned at the end of 1972, thinly disguised Grand Prix machines with all-enveloping bodywork appeared. The Ferrari 312P and Matra V12 were two examples, racing dullards, which by the mid-1970s had been superseded by a gaggle of Porsche 911 derivatives. As the decade wore on, the 911 changed in appearance from the pretty sports/GT, with which everyone was familiar, into a uglier silhouette.

The arrival of the new Group C and C2 classes in the early 1980s was a breath of fresh air. Virtually from the beginning of this new formula, the beautiful Porsche 956 was all-

conquering, dominating the international series for much of the decade.

With Lancia and, later, Jaguar and Daimler-Benz joining the fray, motor-racing fans were treated to a 'golden' period of sports-car racing. Riding high on the efforts and initiative of Swiss, Peter Sauber, whose cars, running with twin-turbocharged Mercedes V8 engines, were showing great promise by 1985, Daimler-Benz threw its weight behind the project. Painted in traditional Mercedes metallic silver, and carrying minimal sponsorship, this new breed of 'Silver Arrows' became, like those before them in the 1930s and 50s, an awe-inspiring sight on the world's race tracks.

In 1989, Daimler-Benz claimed the greatest prize of all – outright victory in the Le Mans 24 Hours – and, in the manner of all the 'greats', made it all look easy. The two leading cars ran like clockwork throughout the 24 hours. Shortly before the finish, they called at the pits, where mechanics wiped away the grime covering the star roundels on the nose cones to emphasize during the final laps that the great Mercedes concern was well and truly back.

Running parallel to the sports-racing programme, Daimler-Benz also fielded a a large number of 190 saloons in the freshly inaugurated German Touring Car Championship (DTM), alongside entrants from Opel, BMW, Alfa-Romeo and Audi. Over many years, all the great factory teams won races, with star drivers thrilling spectators in closely fought battles. The cars were among the most technically advanced and, on circuits like the old Nürburgring, proved themselves capable of speeds of up to 180mph (290km/h).

The DTM not only attracted large crowds of spectators, but was broadcast worldwide on satellite television to an appreciative audience of millions. Enormous publicity was generated by the television coverage, especially for Mercedes, which was more successful in the series than most. The company's investment had more than paid off, and showroom sales escalated. Daimler-Benz began to make make money like never before, its business activities no longer confined to the manufacture of cars and commercial vehicles. Like others of their ilk, the company had become an important, powerful and global player, with huge economic and political influence.

During the 1980s, saloon-car racing and participation in the International Sports Car Championship threw the name of Mercedes into the sporting arena once again. They had started in the same way in the 1950s, with a similar aim – a stab at joining the Formula One procession. When Mercedes returned to Grand Prix racing in 1954, manufacturers built their own cars with their own people. Virtually every component, except the tyres, was made in-house. Sponsorship was provided by companies working within the motor industry, which were noisy about their successes, and silent about less successful ventures. Cars were normally painted in national racing colours – green for Britain, silver for Germany, red for Italy, blue for France, and so on – and sponsors' logos, except in the US, never appeared on bodywork.

By 1967, however, the arrival of the Cosworth DFV ('double four valve') engine in F1 signalled the beginning of the 'kit-car' era. A year later, Lotus boss Colin Chapman painted his cars in the colours of Gold Leaf cigarettes as a means of paying for his team's racing activities. Cigarette smoking had little to do with motor racing, but Chapman's initiative would change the face of competition and of sport in general.

Partnerships between manufacturers and sponsors were forged for the financial health of both, and there were far-reaching consequences. During the 1990s, Daimler-Benz would supply engines, built by Ilmor in Britain, to Ron Dennis's eye-wateringly successful McLaren Formula One team. Mika Hakkinen's victorious back-to-back Champi-

onship titles would bring riches and perpetuate the day-to-day struggle to 'win at any cost'.

Increasingly, even the big players needed business partners to survive in the modern world of 'globalization'. In the mid-1990s, there was a successful merger between Daimler-Benz and Chrysler, creating a new corporation called DaimlerChrysler. This, and the subsequent acquisition of Mitsubishi, demonstrated the need for greater streamlining and efficiency. The enormous cost of developing new models that complied with the legal requirements of so many different markets was escalating year on year. Indeed, it continues to rise.

At the beginning of the twenty-first century, the Mercedes image had completely changed. The range of cars had widened appreciably to include, for the first time, a front-wheel-drive hatchback at one end of the scale, saloons and a four-wheel-drive in the middle, and a supercar at the other extreme. The company promotes a smart lifestyle image, prompted in part by BMW's similar image of many years standing, and investment in motor racing at the highest level, with its perceived glamour, is the most cost-effective means of staying in business.

It was once almost unthinkable that the conservative products of Daimler-Benz would become popular subjects for tuning and customizing by specialist companies, but this is precisely what has happened in the past few years. Mercs with wings, skirts, fat boots and a 'zillion' horsepower provide devotees with very personalized transport, and the 'after-market' industry is worth millions – it has all been born out of Daimler-Benz's long-term investment in motor sport.

The staggering technology to be found in modern Mercedes has many of its roots in the 1970s (*see* Chapter 6), and it is interesting to reflect on a piece headed 'The Trend of Design' by Bill Boddy in the November 1977 issue of *Motor Sport*. Boddy's comments are worthy of lengthy repetition, for they illustrate matters of the moment:

> In spite of all the anti-pollution and fuel conservation restrictions, automobile design shows little curbing of initiative. The diesel engine, which *Motor Sport* has advocated, is making surprisingly good headway, led by Volkswagen's noteworthy contribution. Mercedes-Benz, in this field, and Audi in the petrol-engine sphere, have introduced in-line 5-cylinder power units, and Colt have resorted to using a modern version of of the Lanchester Harmonic Balancer to smooth out their 4-cylinder power packs.
>
> Light alloy retains its worthwhile place in engine manufacture, particularly at Rover's, the classic twin-cam valvegear still finds its place under the bonnets of certain models made by Alfa Romeo, Fiat, Jaguar, Lotus, Mercedes-Benz and Toyota, and catalogue mid-engined coupés are multiplying satisfactorily. However, anyone who has read about the way in which the Ford Fiesta was planned and developed will have no illusions about the importance now being placed on styling, by the big motor manufacturers engaged in the top sales-rat-race.

Boddy went on to discuss safety in motor cars – the other burning issue of the day – and quoted the great Italian designer Sergio Pininfarina, who believed that total safety is not achievable and, maybe, is not even necessary. According to Pininfarina, 'The great majority of accidents which cause death and injuries happen at speeds lower than the one prescribed by the ESV technical specifications.'

In the ensuing years, Daimler-Benz and the majority of other manufacturers have made 'mainstream' cars aesthetically more appealing (though not in all cases), and considerably safer, thanks largely to the pioneering techniques developed by Daimler-Benz. However, people have continued to have accidents.

With the benefit of hindsight, Mercedes, Porsche, BMW and Volkswagen all rose to the considerable challenges of the 1970s, and have made unrivalled progress since.

In that November 1977 *Motor Sport* article, Bill Boddy also made the following comments:

> It is sad news for Britain in general and Jaguar enthusiasts in particular that the two Jaguar sports/racing coupés have been abandoned by Leyland Cars, without gaining a single race victory (but a second at the Nürburgring), and after experiencing a most unfortunate string of retirements. Except, of course, that the cost, variously estimated at from £250,000 to £500,000, is public money, from which some of the 'shareholders' might have wished for a better return.

Although these words were published a quarter of a century ago, during which so many things have changed in the motor industry, there are certain facets of British manufacturing that remain the same, while Germany moves on and on and on...

6 S Club 1972–80

Codenamed 'W116' in Daimler-Benz's ostensibly logical numbering system, work began on the superb S-Class in the mid-1960s, the range making its public debut in 1972. It was, and remains, one of the finest, safest and most impressive saloons, and it is surely a testament to the quality of Mercedes engineering that there are still so many examples in regular use today.

Natural competitors included the Rolls-Royce Silver Shadow, Jaguar XJ6 and later XJ12, Citroën–Maserati SM and BMW 2500/2800 Series. All of these cars were expensive to buy and maintain, and combined luxury with performance, safety and fine road manners. Regrettably, the Jaguar's career was blighted by the mess that British Leyland became, but not before *Motor Sport* had declared the 3.4-litre car 'excellent value for money'.

The Citroën was delightfully 'quirky' – a lovely classic – but front-wheel-drive and mechanical complexity was not to everyone's taste. The Silver Shadow appealed to Rolls' usual clientele, and the BMW never failed to impress. Even in this hallowed company, however, the S-Class Mercedes stood head and shoulders above the rest.

In the summer of 1975, Stirling Moss and Denis Jenkinson set out on an epic journey in a 450SE. Their aim was to re-trace the same route they had taken in 1955 on their famous and victorious outing on the Mille Miglia in

The W116 S-Class debuted at the Paris Motor Show in 1972; it stunned those present and redefined luxury saloon motoring.

A great deal of research and development work led to the creation of the world's safest saloon. Despite its large dimensions, it was also extremely handsome.

the 300SLR sports-racing car. A piece by Alan Henry was published in *Motor Sport* shortly after:

Our schedules obliged us to exchange nostalgia for reality and we were soon speeding effortlessly down the *autobahn* towards Munich in the air-conditioned luxury of the 450SE saloon, this beautifully contrived and superbly finished executive express content to cruise for hours at a stretch at 120mph [195km/h] and returning something around 15mpg [19l/100km] whilst doing so.

Many of Europe's long-distance motorways are tedious grinds to the Continental traveller, but this route up over the Brenner and down into northern Italy provides spectacular scenery and splendour which is well worth seeing. Round the tight,

The frontal aspect was shark-like, with a grille that was lower than on its predecessor, giving greater aerodynamic efficiency.

sweeping curves, the 450SE seemed stable and confident, the spirited rasp of a Swiss-registered Dino 308 coupé on the inside of a tight curve heralding the only car to pass us between Innsbruck and Trento, the first major town on the Italian side of the border.

It was exactly this kind of motoring for which the S-Class was built, and of course, it excelled itself in every way. It is interesting to record, however, just how much motoring had changed in twenty years. According to Alan Henry, 'Pressing on in the 450SE, we reached Ravenna in four hours' fairly enthusiastic

Below *The body was wedge-shaped, and lower at the front than at the rear. By the 1970s, improved fuel consumption and cleaner exhaust emissions had become universally important, and the development of aerodynamically efficient bodywork was one way of aiding both.*

The rear was lean and large, giving an impression of power and unrivalled purpose. Despite the width of the car, though, passengers had less room inside because of massive side-impact beams in the doors.

motoring.' The Moss and Jenkinson 300SLR had completed the same distance in 1955 in 1 hour 36 minutes! Even more sobering is the fact that it took Moss and Jenks a little over 10 hours to complete the 1,000-mile course in 1955, while taking a modern, powerful 450SE over the same route in 1975 took three and half days.

How long would the same journey take today in a modern Mercedes?

Behind Benign Energy

A large, purposeful-looking motor car, the W116 had a typically Teutonic frontal appearance. It looked as though it would never suffer fools gladly and, as it turned out, this image was spot on. Few remained indifferent to the styling; observers either loved it or hated it. Luckily for Daimler-Benz, nearly half a mil-

Below *The steel hull was torsionally more rigid than on all previous Mercedes saloons, and the entire structure easily exceeded the requirements of US legislation in crash testing.*

The roof pillars were reinforced to withstand heavy, high-speed impacts, but invited criticism from some journalists because of their width.

lion people voted in the car's favour with their large wallets.

In line with typical Daimler-Benz principles, under chief engineer Hans Scherenberg, the body was long and low and, because of safety considerations, much heavier than that of the previous S-Class. The car's structural integrity was unrivalled; all impact zones had been strengthened or reinforced, and external visual evidence of this was readily apparent in the shape and thickness of the roof pillars. Additional strengthening of the four doors gave passengers greater protection against side impacts than in any other car, but there was a small penalty to pay in decreased elbow space.

Naturally, the centre section of the car was a rigid cell, designed to absorb shock loading after the front or rear crumple areas had taken the brunt of a collision. *Motor Sport* felt that 'the exceptional safety aspects of this 16.27ft long body [were] widely enough known not to require detailing'. The reporter went on to claim, 'If you're going to have an accident you're more likely to survive in the 450SE than possibly any other car in the world.' The same principles applied to other models in the range.

The bodyshell was shaped in a wind tunnel, according to sound aerodynamic principles. This new thinking had largely been dictated by considerations regarding fuel consumption, and even more so after the 1973 oil crisis, which is why the W116 was slightly wedge-shaped. (British Leyland took this wedge approach to extremes with its Ambassador/Princess, which proved to be wildly short of the mark.)

Angled upwards, the sill and upright of the rear side windows were shaped to reduce aerodynamic drag and wind noise, and to prevent draughts. Again, this kind of attention to detail justifies the relatively high purchase price of a Mercedes.

Headlamps and indicator units had a rather sinister appearance, a styling touch appreciated by BMW, whose pretty 6-cylinder saloons were gaining ground rapidly on their Stuttgart rivals.

At the front of the big Merc, the headlamps and parking lights were enclosed by a single lens that flanked the huge chromium-plated radiator grille. The star motif on top of the grille was designed to flip backwards in the event of contact with a high-speed human, or anything else.

Motor Sport had a pithy remark to make: 'Apart from the boot-lid badge the only detail which signifies the depth of one's wallet appears to be the 450SE's growth of wipers and washers for the curved lenses of the huge, rectangular, halogen headlights.' Such luxury items were novel at the time, but many commentators considered them to be essential for road safety.

Curiously, the heavy, fluted bonnet was hinged at the rear. Front and rear there were the familiar double-bladed bumpers, capped

Below *Brightwork covers over the wheel arches were popular in the 1970s but tended to trap moisture and cause rusting. The tail lamps and indicators had 'stepped' lenses to minimize a build-up of road grime.*

Traditional 'clap-hands' windscreen wipers gave way to modern, parallel items that gave a huge sweep of the screen,

with rubber strips to protect pedestrians. The same style of 'stripping' was applied to the flanks to protect the sheet metal, and to break up the vast expanse of bodywork. With nicely rounded 'shoulders' to the sides, though, there was nothing 'slab-sided' about the design.

Although smaller in volume than on the previous S-Class, the boot was cavernous, and Mercedes also provided a warning triangle on the underside of the boot lid (although the reliability of the cars meant that it was unlikely to be used much).

The most striking feature of the tail was the wide lamp lenses, which were 'stepped'. The aim of this unique Mercedes design was to keep parts of the 'segmented' plastic clean and visible in inclement weather. Apart from their

Below *It was typical of Daimler-Benz that in standard form the S-Class was fitted with steel road wheels embellished with colour-keyed hubcaps. Alloy wheels, which considerably improved overall looks, were expensive extra-cost options.*

Although leather was an extra-cost option, the standard seats were in velour and most comfortable. Legroom was generous, and the true comfort of the S-Class was best appreciated after a journey of several hundreds of miles.

practical value these tail lamps provided a strong styling tenet; a similar design was used on Daimler-Benz's commercial fleet, making the less glamorous vehicles instantly distinguishable from the herd.

Bright trim was much in evidence and still in vogue in the luxury-car market, despite a definite departure from such decadence in sports-car design.

Motor Sport could not resist a jibe, pointing out that 'petrol pump attendants complained about the fuel filler flap being hinged at the bottom so that the strong spring fought with the filler nozzle or had to be repelled with one hand. The flap's paintwork was chipped as a result.' The same magazine complained that the nearside front door 'fitted fairly badly', which is hard to believe, in view of the way in which the factory at Sindelfingen is organized. Dr Sodt did move in mysterious ways, however, as demonstrated by the following anecdote.

A few years ago, I accompanied a couple of friends to the factory in Stuttgart to take delivery of two brand-new cars. My role was to photograph and record this minor event, and the return trip, for a magazine. Within less than ten miles of leaving the factory, one of the cars had developed faults. The carpet in the passenger footwell was awash with an unidentified fluid, and the front nearside indicator assembly had fallen on to the road and smashed into a thousand pieces. Under normal circumstances it would be more or less impossible to dislodge an indicator unit, but this one had simply fallen out, perhaps because there was a journalist with a camera in the back seat!

The W116 had screen-pillar deflectors to keep the side windows free of road grime, but just one door-mounted aerodynamically

shaped rear-view mirror. An additional one on the passenger door was an extra-cost option, and some considered this to be a grave omission on Mercedes' part.

In standard guise the cars were fitted with pressed-steel wheels, and hubcaps in body colour with a chromed band and star motif. Their appearance was smart, conservative, and Germanically Mercedes; in essence, the style had not changed for many years. The alternative, a set of attractive alloys to the same design as those introduced on the 280SL sports car in 1969, gave the grand machines a more purposeful appearance.

Internal Examination

Apart from its sheer size, the interior was as

Above *In characteristic fashion the facia, instruments and controls were well laid out, aesthetically dull and primarily built with driver and passenger safety in mind. The steering wheel was as large as ever.*

Left *The majority of cars were fitted with automatic transmission, but the lever, 'gate' and surrounding veneer trim left a great deal to be desired from an aesthetic point of view. Frankly, the wood veneer did not look well.*

They were practical and utilitarian, but the ventilation outlets on the extremities of the dashboard, coupled with the wood veneer, gave the appearance of an unfinished refrigerator.

Below *In contrast with the facia, the interior door panelling (shown here in vinyl and velour) was practical and stylish. Side-impact beams, however, left little space for storing oddments in the well of the door.*

safe as it could possibly be at the time. The car's weight and size ensured that anyone colliding with an S-Class was going to come off second best, but the occupants of the Merc were also well looked after. Virtually every surface was padded, and a comprehensive first-aid kit was provided. (Incidentally, the carrying of a first-aid kit had become a legal requirement in

mainland Europe long before British manufacturers even thought about providing one.)

Both the front and rears doors were large enough to allow easy access, and large, firmly padded seats provided armchair-like comfort.

Despite the efforts of the designers, *Motor Sport* found plenty to criticize:

Much as I like leather, I think I would have rejected this £450 extra in the test car in favour of standard cloth; the material compounded the inherent hardness of the Mercedes seating and the stitching of the pleating showed a standard of workmanship somewhat lower than that employed by Jaguar's trimming department. The individual front seats are generously proportioned, split by an armrest which can be folded out of the way and the driver's seat can be adjusted for height as well as reach and rake. Perversely, the knurled knob rake adjusters both face the inside, right beneath the armrest hinge and against the centre tunnel, almost inaccessible. Some of the plastic bits used in the interior are positively Ford-like, particularly the plastic cover over the passenger seat hinge mecha-

Passenger comfort has not been improved upon in modern Mercs, which is one reason for the genuine classic status of the 1970s S-Class.

nism, which continually fell off in the test car. The loop-pile carpet had none of the look of quality one would expect in the price of the car.

The poor carpeting in the 280SL had also been subjected to similar vitriol; it would last just about for ever, which saves money for people restoring the cars today, but it remains visually unappealing.

Surprisingly, the massive steering wheel was not adjustable. It also featured a huge padded boss, but no one could argue about its safety aspect, or its comfort in use.

Instrumentation was spartan, with just three principal gauges – a central speedometer flanked by a noisy clock and combination gauge – feeding adequate information to the driver. A tachometer would have been a useful substitute for the clock, but the former was not fitted to cars exported to Britain.

All switchgear was within easy reach, made of soft plastics and, as far as was practicably possible, tucked out of harm's way. Useful stowage bins in the doors, an oddments tray on the centre console and stowage nets on the backs of the front seats were typical of German functionalism. A radio/cassette player was an extra-cost option, and those provided by dealers were usually from Blaupunkt. (The cassette player in *Motor Sport*'s test car, incidentally, played at twice the normal speed.)

280S (W116) 1972–80

Unitary construction four-door saloon

Engine

Cylinders	6
Bore × stroke	86mm × 78.8mm
Capacity	2746cc
Timing	Twin-overhead camshafts
Compression ratio	9:1
Carburettor	Solex 4A1
Max power	160bhp at 5,500rpm
Max torque	166.4lb ft at 4,000rpm

Transmission

Gearbox	4-speed manual, 5-speed manual, automatic

Ratios 4-speed manual

First	3.90:1
Second	2.30:1
Third	1.41:1
Fourth	1:1
Reverse	3.66:1

Ratios 4-speed automatic

First	3.98:1
Second	2.39:1
Third	1.46:1
Fourth	1:1
Reverse	5.48:1

Ratios 5-speed manual

First	3.96:1
Second	2.34:1
Third	1.43:1
Fourth	1:1
Fifth	0.88:1
Reverse	3.72:1

Suspension and steering

Front	Unequal-length wishbones, coil springs and auxiliary rubber springs, hydraulic dampers and anti-roll bar
Rear	Semi-trailing arms, coil springs with auxiliary rubber springs, hydraulic telescopic dampers and anti-roll bar
Steering	Power-assisted recirculating ball

Brakes

Dual-circuit servo-assisted discs all round

Dimensions

Track	(front) 60in (1500 mm) (rear) 59.3in (1482.5mm)
Wheelbase	112.8in (2820mm)
Overall length	195.3in (4882.5mm)
Overall width	73.4in (1835mm)
Overall height	56.1in (1402.5mm)

Both manual and automatic had the shift lever on the central tunnel, column changes finally banished, and although left-hookers all had foot-operated parking brakes, right-hand drives came with the traditional umbrella-style lever mounted under the dashboard.

No one found fault with the heating and ventilation systems but, for £755 and £276 extra respectively, the buyer could have air-conditioning or an electrically operated sunroof.

Most of the interior equipment present in the S-Class made good sense and, although the 'luxury' items of the 1970s are taken for granted today, the Mercedes was a state-of-the-art motor vehicle on its launch at the Paris Motor Show in 1972. Journalists on both sides of the Atlantic frequently expressed surprise at the spartan nature of the interior; they thought that a car that was so expensive should have been stuffed with gauges, handles, whistles, levers and gadgets that were likely to make an impression on the neighbours. In reality, the Mercedes did have all the features found on contemporary Jaguars and the rest, but they were less overtly on display. This was a deliberate move on the part of Mercedes' designers. To them, the main purpose of a car is to transport people. Daimler-Benz (along with BMW) believes that people should be carried in the safest and best way possible, without stress, distraction or want, so interior design is kept as simple as needs dictate.

Send in the Clones

Built to the same standard and clothed in the same garments, the model range was introduced piecemeal with a choice of 6- and 8-cylinder engines. Initially, this choice

These hugely impressive beasts were available with 2.8-, 3.5, 4.5- or 6.9-litre engines; put another way, they were quick, fast, faster or utterly mind-blowing.

Apart from its impressive looks and presence, the big S-Class was a true driver's car, with cornering ability and performance second to none in the luxury bracket. Even at top speed, the car was so smooth and quiet that it was easy to gain the impression that walking would have been quicker.

<table>
<tr><td colspan="2">350SE (W116) 1972–80</td></tr>
</table>

350SE (W116) 1972–80

Specification as for 280S except for the following:

Engine

Cylinders	V8
Bore × stroke	92mm × 65.8mm
Capacity	3499cc
Timing	Single-overhead camshaft per bank
Compression ratio	9.5:1
Fuel system	Bosch D-Jetronic fuel injection
Max power	200bhp at 5,800rpm, 205bhp at 5,750rpm form January 1978
Max torque	204lb ft at 4,000rpm, 203lb ft at 4,000rpm from January 1978

Gearbox

	4-speed synchromesh manual
Ratios	3.96:1
Second	2.34:1
Third	1.43:1
Fourth	1:1
Reverse	3.72:1

Optional 3-speed automatic
Ratios

First	2.31:1
Second	1.46:1
Third	1:1
Reverse	1.84:1

450SE (W116) 1972–80

Specification as for 350SE except as follows:

Engine

Cylinders	V8
Bore × stroke	92mm × 85mm
Capacity	4502cc
Compression ratio	8.8:1
Fuel system	Bosch D-Jetronic fuel injection, K-Jetronic from mechanical fuel injection from November 1975
Max power	225bhp at 5,000rpm
Max torque	278.5lb ft at 3,000rpm

450SEL 6.9 1975–80

Specification as for 450SE except as follows:

Engine

Cylinders	V8
Bore × stroke	107mm × 95mm
Capacity	6834cc
Compression ratio	8.8:1
Max power	286bhp at 4,250rpm
Max torque	405lb ft at 3,000rpm

Suspension
Self-levelling hydro-pneumatic springs with gas-filled dampers front and rear

was limited to the familiar twin-carburettor double-overhead camshaft 2746cc 6-cylinder 280S, fuel-injection 280SE or 3499cc V8, also with fuel injection, in the 350SE. The 4.5- and 6.3-litre versions of the 450SE were launched in 1973.

Differences in performance among the models were slight, the main advantage with the larger-engined cars being increased quantities of torque. Standstill to 60mph with the 280SE took 9.8 seconds, while the 450SE could accomplish the same dash in 9 seconds.

Frankly, from the driver's seat it would have been virtually impossible to tell the difference. At 7 seconds, the later 6.9-litre car was quick by any standards, but overall fuel consumption of 14mpg (20.25l/100km), although good for the engine capacity, was anti-social. (James Hunt, 1976 Formula One Champion, owned one of these magnificent flagships but, even with his income, the car spent much of its time on the driveway, propped up on bricks.)

In the middle ground the 350SE was capable of flat-out motoring at around

Revised suspension – wishbones up front and semi-trailing arms at the rear – gave much more neutral handling characteristics. Swing-axle rear suspension was finally dropped, and journalists the world over were finally silenced.

123mph (197km/h), while the 4.5-litre version could hit 135mph (216km/h), respectable figures considering the car's overall weight of nearly 4,000lb (1820kg). A long-wheelbase 450SEL, with an extra 4in (100mm), was launched in 1973 and, from 1974, there were also long-wheel-base versions of the 2.8- and 3.5-litre cars.

Journalists and owners found little to gripe about. There was certainly induction noise under heavy acceleration, slight wind and tyre noise, but *Motor Sport* found the 450SE to offer 'total insulation, a cocoon of silence'.

Clive Richardson also made the following comments in *Motor Sport*:

Off-the-line performance is disappointing, over 3.5 seconds taken from zero to 30mph, a penalty

of high gearing and the physical effort of givng this heavy car some inertia. It was interesting in this respect to compare the 450SE with our managing director's 280SE 3.5, now with some 80,000 reliable miles on the clock, yet little sign of age. This lighter, low-geared car felt much quicker off the line, right up to the middle ranges, when the extra power, torque and improved streamlining took the new car galloping ahead. It is in these middle and upper ranges, rather than in sheer standing-start acceleration, that the 450SE excels, all-powerfully, simply 'whooshing' through overtaking. The

Power outputs ranged from 160bhp at 5,500rpm in the carburetted 6-cylinder 280S to 286bhp at 4,250rpm in the 6.9-litre V8 version of the 450SEL. Exhaust-emissions equipment inhibited the potential power of the superbly made engines.

engine is by no means silent when pressed like this, though the gruff rumble from underbonnet is well enough muted.

Daimler-Benz's power units were as dependable and as beautifully made as the rest of the car. The sum of these parts had clearly result-ed in the best saloon in the world, a title it would hold until 1988 when BMW's E34 5 Series would take on this illustrious mantle.

All the Other Bits

The W116's suspension, in conjunction with power-assisted recirculating-ball steering, gave handling qualities in dry weather which some regarded as definitive. With so much weight, care had to be exercised in the wet, because at high speed the car gave the impres-sion of merely ambling along.

Up front were the usual wishbones, coil springs and anti-roll bar, but with telescopic shock absorbers fitted outboard of the

The natural habitat of the S-Class was the motorway, where it could demonstrate its speed and comfort. These cars will probably be regarded one day as the spiritual successors to the great pre-war SSK series.

springs. Weight savings had reduced unsprung weight, and anti-dive geometry – in effect, front and rear – curtailed the tendency of these powerful machines to squat hard under acceleration and pitch downwards under heavy braking. At the rear there were semi-trailing arms, coil springs, telescopic dampers and an anti-roll bar. Braking was by vented discs at the front and solids at the rear, and no one, including *Motor Sport*'s Clive Richardson, could knock them: 'They stop this heavy machine from single-figure or three-figure speeds with the same sensational lack of drama thanks to their power and the anti-dive action of the suspension.'

Like some contemporary BMWs, the Merc had a tendency momentarily to spin its rear wheels on damp surfaces, which a limit-ed-slip differential would have negated. It was not possible to have everything, even in a Mercedes-Benz S-Class that, in the mid-

1970s, cost nearly three times as much as the average semi-detached house.

Power-assisted steering – standard across the range – was hailed by journalists on both sides of the Atlantic as the best in the world, allowing for superb directional control and first-rate 'feedback' from the road.

Both manual and automatic transmission were available, the former proving the most popular in North America. Development and refinement had banished the 'clunkiness' for which Daimler-Benz's automatics had once been noted, and the W116's transmission was univerally praised for its brilliance. *Motor Sport*'s Clive Richardson was unequivocal in his praise:

> I must give credit to the Mercedes automatic gear-box. This three-speed box is so smooth and quiet, is so sensibly behaved in traffic (I abhor boxes which are forever changing up and down in these conditions) and has a splendid kick-down arrangement which allows selection of intermediate to hasten overtaking acceleration from below 85mph [135km/h], or, with the lever in Drive, to kick-down into Low below 41mph. In the Intermediate hold position, kick-down will select Low below 47mph [65.5km/h], a most useful facility in hilly country. In fact I used this hold far less than I do with most automatics, for this gearbox has such ideal characteristics when left to its own devices. Like that of the SL, the gearbox was slow to take up in reverse.

Despite the oil crisis of 1973, the lowest-powered 280SE sold less well than the other cars in the range. Although fuel-rationing in Britain and much of mainland Europe spread an aura of gloom – some even considered that the end of the motor car was in sight – research and development continued unabated. While the oil crisis put paid to BMW's thirsty 2002 turbo, and the Munich company temporarily axed its magnificent V12 power unit (although a

revised version would appear in the late 1980s), Daimler-Benz pressed ahead with a new eye-opener in 1975.

The New Project
Publicly debuted at the 1975 Frankfurt Motor Show, the 450SEL 6.9 (6843cc) was an ambitious project that, in one sense, flew in the face of contemporary common sense. Not even Daimler-Benz's clever engineers could make such a large-capacity engine fuel-thrifty, but this was their business, and that of customers to whom money was little or no object. As the previous 6.3-litre flagship had proved, there was a ready market for a top-notch 'super-limo' with electrifying dynamics. Former chief development engineer Rudi Uhlenhaut had always insisted that, in any case, it was much easier to design and build complex cars rather than simple inexpensive ones.

The car was aimed at well-heeled hot-shots who needed supercar performance with the luxury of the 600 Pullman, but without the latter's inhibiting dimensions. Created by special projects man Eric Waxenberger, who was possessed of a heavy right foot and sufficient skill to use it, the new car retailed in Britain at £24,000. To put this figure into perspective, the Jaguar XJ12 cost £11,880!

In 1978, *The Motor*'s reporter filed an article headed 'If seven is heaven, what's 6.9?'. He said, 'Make no mistake, the 6.9 is one of the world's great cars but it is also cool on character and not as close to perfection as I suspect Uhlenhaut would have liked for the price. At least, that's what my filed test notes suggest.'

The V8 6.9-litre was essentially a 'bored-out' version of the previous 6.3-litre unit, with dry-sump lubrication, self-adjusting tappets and Bosch K-Jetronic mechanical fuel injection. Externally, the car could be distinguished from the 4.5-litre model by a discreet '6.9' badge on the boot lid, and fatter tyres. Its other

distinguishing feature was an additional £8,000 on the showroom price tag.

It's difficult, or even impossible, to judge whether or not Daimler-Benz had set out with the aim of producing the ultimate sporting saloon of the day. There is no doubt, though, that the 6.9 was in a class of its own. Unlike contemporaries from Britain and America, the Mercedes was more likely to impress a driver than, perhaps, its passengers. Natural rivals included the Silver Shadow, Bristol 412, Vanden Plas Daimler and Cadillac Seville. *The Motor* also mentioned the Panther de Ville, a 'retro' creation designed to resemble a Type 41 Bugatti Royale, and powered by a V12 Jaguar engine. At £41, 417, the Panther was almost double the price of the 6.9 Mercedes, twice as vulgar, and almost incapable of justifying its existence.

With 286bhp and 405lb ft of torque, the Merc's 6.9-litre engine drove through a three-speed automatic gearbox and standard ZF limited-slip differential. With a top speed of 143.9mph (230.25km/h) and 0–60mph potential of 7.9 seconds, it outperformed all its rivals, except the lighter, alloy-bodied Bristol. Although the 6.3-litre Mercedes was quicker from 0–60mph, the new car was carrying 2 tons, an apparent lack of progress in this department being excusable on the grounds of safety.

A number of 6.9s were also armour-plated, the additional weight having little effect on the car's performance.

Of its ability to travel forwards quickly, *The Motor* made the following comments:

> The performance is shattering. Although 286bhp may seem a mite modest for an injected 6.9-litre OHC V8, red-lined at a lowly 5,000rpm, the

Opposite *Today, prices for the S-Class are at rock bottom, and several examples languish in fields or barns, rotting or awaiting restoration. For enthusiasts, they are there for the taking.*

colossal 405lb ft of torque certainly isn't. Mighty Merc accelerates with a seething surge that is never less than serene to reach 60mph in 7.5 seconds, 100 in under 20, and we timed it at 144mph [230km/h] in Germany. In favourable conditions it is said to be capable of 150mph [240km/h], so before any Porsche and Ferrari drivers trifle with a 450, they should ensure that it doesn't have a 6.9 tail badge.

This was, of course, the whole point of this elitest limo. It simply dispelled the myth that quick, nimble handlers only came in the form of a Dino or a Carrera. Mercedes had demonstrated similar prowess before the war with the SSK models, and continues in the same mould today with the V12.

Road Contact

In another attempt to 'reinvent' the coil spring, the suspension system was similar to the previous air-suspension type, but with nitrogen cylinders, oil-filled struts and gas-filled shock absorbers. The nitrogen bags were held under pressure by a pump driven by the engine. Although more reliable than the old system and less prone to leaks, it was complex and led to some colourful language among mechanics when its bits and pieces failed to work properly. However, it did allow for superb handling and ride, even if the latter was not quite in the class of the Silver Shadow. Most were agreed that the power-assisted steering could not be bettered, but the old Mercedes chestnut – an overly large steering wheel – drew criticism as usual. Mercedes was quite big enough to ignore vitriol in this respect.

The suspension, in conjunction with the steering, led *The Motor* to comment that 'big saloons don't normally excel on tight, twisty roads but the 6.9 loves them'. The reporter went to say, 'Poise and predictability are expected of a Mercedes. But such agility from a 2-ton heavyweight borders on the uncanny.

Citroën could learn a thing or two from its pitch and roll damping, and anti-squat and dive geometry that keeps the Mercedes on an even keel however hard you accelerate, brake or corner.'

As with all other cars of this era with an abundance of power and weight, a lack of respect or wanton recklessness could result in a rude awakening. To quote *The Motor* again:

> If the 6.9 has a flaw here it is that it could flatter the unskilled into a false sense of security. Even on respectable Michelin tyres of 215 section, imprudent use of the accelerator can induce violent wheelspin on a wet road and unleash the tail into a spectacular powerslide. It is all very controllable but a sideways 6.9 takes up a lot of road! Intended or provoked, it is the relative ease with which traction can be broken that is the only weakness in Mighty Merc's otherwise impeccable road manners.

The same writer went on to knock the car's 'inability' to deal with irregularities in the road surface, its wind noise at high speeds, the hiss from the interior air vents and the need to increase the volume of the radio above 100mph (160km/h). Although perfectly justifiable criticisms, these gripes simply showed that this journalist was missing the point. For 'performance in peace', he recommended a Jaguar XJ12, a car that made a lot of noise, but protected its occupants from any racket in the finest manner. But would it start every time?

The Motor's report came to the following conclusion:

> Stunning yes, sensuous no. If you happen to want a big, bland unpretentious slingshot that feels as if it's been carved from the solid and can be thrown around like a Mini, I can suggest nothing better than a 6.9 SEL. But despite its many great qualities, notably its phenomenal performance and handling, Mighty Merc is more likely to command your respect than to capture your heart.

This was not the first or last time a British publication would offer the view that German cars lacked 'spirit'. Some German cars may not have had the beauty of pre-war Alfa Romeos and some post-war Ferraris, but the 6.9 was designed for a specific purpose – transporting people at high speed in the safest possible way. In this role, it acquitted itself better than most. Surely it was no coincidence that several Grand Prix drivers of the day favoured these cars.

Image Burner

The W116, one of Daimler-Benz's finest ever cars, made a huge impact on those who owned and drove it. In 1977, the company introduced a diesel version for the North American market. A turbocharged 3-litre producing a paltry 115bhp, but capable of returning 27mpg, the 300SD was a huge success in a country that was just waking up to the need to conserve future fuel supplies.

The idea of an S-Class with a diesel engine, let alone one that developed less in the way of horsepower than a 'cooking' family saloon with a 2-litre petrol engine, was absurd, but peculiarly successful. Diesels were becoming popular in America, purely because of the greater economy they offererd. With development they would also produce real performance, but still at the expense of contaminating the air with sooty particulates.

The 300SD was as well equipped in most respects as the regular petrol-engined W116 range, but there was no getting away from the engine's comparative lack of refinement. Since this time, Mercedes cars with turbo-diesel engines have become as commonplace around the world as their 'atmo' counterparts had in

Opposite *The passage of more than thirty years since the debut of the S-Class has done nothing to dim the excitement the car generates. Launched today, it would still look fresh and appealing.*

previous years. They may be practical, but some would argue that they do little for the company's image.

Once Great Cars...

The W116 enjoyed a fruitful production life of seven years, the average lifespan of any car before being replaced. A truly classic vehicle, by any standards, this version of the S-Class was in some senses the inevitable result of 1960s thinking, and, in some quarters, hysteria.

The series embraced the widely held view that the motor industry needed to take responsibility for car safety. No company did more than Daimler–Benz to advance the theme but its high levels of safety were achieved through a tank-like build. Weight had been added to protect the cabin's occupants during collision, and heavy fuel consumption was the inevitable penalty.

From the end of the 1970s, the W116 was replaced by the W126, which was much lighter, but equally safe. In many respects it was an improved car, but its softer body lines were undistinguished in comparison with the classic 1970s Teuton.

7   Loud Volume Market

The W123

The launch of the 5 Series BMW in 1972, and the Munich company's highly successful 3 Series just three years later, made a significant impact on the board of Daimler–Benz. The

The compact W123 saloon replaced the W114/115 range in 1976, and was a much-improved car. Safer and more technically advanced, this entry-level Mercedes broadened the appeal of the range considerably.

threat to the supremacy of Mercedes from BMW had been many years in the making, and Munich had finally pounced.

The response from Stuttgart was a new range of 200s, or W123s in the official numbering system, launched in 1976. There was little, if nothing, wrong with the outgoing W114/115 model, which was selling in ever-increasing numbers, but the company had to be seen to be pushing forwards in an automotive world that was changing out of all recognition.

Styling was as conservative as ever but neatly executed, and clearly aimed at a middle-class clientele who had yet to accept the more sporting BMWs as an alternative.

Inevitably, BMW's attention to detail and build quality in its products had raised the stakes. This, coupled with Mercedes' constant striving for improvement, led to the creation of a new mid-range saloon. There were seven models in the range: the 200D, 240D and 300D diesels, and 200, 230, 250 and 280E petrol-engined cars. Testing the 280E, *Motor Sport* reported in 1977 on 'perhaps the best looking of all Mercedes saloons', a 'baby S-Class in looks', that made up for in its sheer lack of performance with 'superb road manners and convenient compactness'.

The company had made heavy investment in this model. An increased number of mechanical robots were employed to assemble bodyshells, with the result that all the seam welds were more accurate and consistent. Such new technology brought the factory bang up to date, at a time when British Leyland was working in what amounted to a chaotic car museum, despite huge injections of taxpayers' cash. Having recovered from the after-effects of the 1973 oil crisis, the German car industry was thriving; Britain's was sliding into the abyss, while the Japanese continued to beaver away.

Daimler-Benz's huge investment in the W123 was typically German. In addition to the regular saloons and coupés, an estate would soon join the range. Brilliantly designed and beautifully executed, the new car was safer than the outgoing one, being stronger, torsionally more rigid and easier to maintain and service.

As *Motor Sport* pointed out,: 'Something in the looks of a Mercedes always epitomizes solid, reliable, brilliant engineering and this 280E is no exception. That appearances reflect

200 (W123) 1976–05

Unitary construction four-door saloon

Engine
Cylinders	4
Bore × stroke	87mm × 83.6mm
Capacity	1988cc
Timing	Single-overhead camshaft
Compression ratio	9:1
Carburettor	Stromberg 175CDT
Max power	94bhp at 4,800rpm
Max torque	113lb ft at 3,000rpm

Transmission
Gearbox	4-speed synchromesh manual
Gear ratios	
First	3.90:1
Second	2.30:1
Third	1·41·1
Fourth	1:1
Reverse	3.66:1

Optional 4-speed automatic
Gear ratios	
First	3.98:1
Second	2.39:1
Third	1.46:1
Fourth	1:1
Reverse	5.48:1
Final-drive	3.92:1

Suspension and steering
Front	Double wishbones, coil springs, hydraulic dampers and anti-roll bar
Rear	Semi-trailing arms, coil springs, hydraulic dampers and anti-roll bar. Optional hydro-pneumatic self-levelling
Steering	Power-assisted (optional) recirculating ball

Brakes Dual-circuit servo-assisted discs all round

Dimensions
Track	(front) 58.6in (1465mm) (rear) 56.9in (1422.5mm)
Wheelbase	110in (2750mm)
Overall length	186in (4650mm)
Overall width	70.3in (1757.5mm)
Overall height	56.6in (1415mm)

fact is obvious the moment the key is turned in the driver's door lock: each door's locking button rises silently and smoothly as the vacuum-powered central locking system is activated. The boot lid and petrol filler cap are included in the system, the best in the business.'

Something of a 'watershed' model, the W123 sat midway between the 'old' word and today's sophisticates. In design terms it displayed all the usual Mercedes hallmarks.

Striking Balance

In many respects, the new car set new standards – as BMW's 5 Series had – even if you had to be a devotee of the three-pointed star to accept that the body styling was beautiful. Above all, it looked unmistakably like a Mer-

cedes-Benz. It was something of a scaled-down S-Class, with well-balanced body lines, wider track and wheels, and prominent twin headlamps – perhaps inspired by BMW. The slightly 'wedge-shaped' stance gave an overall appearance that was both modern and purposeful. It could not be described as sporting in the Munich sense, but it was well suited to the traditional conservative tastes of the company's clientele.

The front featured the traditional chromed radiator, which was wider than on the previous model, with a prominent star motif on the top and an additional opening for cool air below the bumper. Although as strong and robust as ever, the bumper, front and rear, had a much less heavy appearance. Stylish 'tapered' flutes on the bonnet completed a frontal picture of restrained elegance.

The glass area was predictably large, and the roof pillars commendably strong, while the flanks were adorned with bright strips and the

Optional alloy wheels transformed the car's looks, and gave the range-topping 280E – capable of 120mph (195km/h) – a class edge.

230 (W123) 1976–81

Specification as for 200 except for the following:

Engine
Cylinders	4
Bore × stroke	93.75mm × 83.6mm
Capacity	2307cc
Compression ratio	9:1
Carburettor	Stromberg 175CDT
Max power	109bhp at 4,800rpm
Max torque	132lb ft at 3,000rpm

wings with discreet flares. At the rear, the boot was typically capable of swallowing the entire contents of a small house, and the lenses of the tail lamps were 'stepped' in the same style as the S-Class.

In standard form the wheels were in steel, and fitted with attractive trims emblazoned with the star motif at their centre. Alloys were equally attractive alternatives, but only available at extra cost.

Research Shows...

The majority of journalists who tested these cars when they were new fundamentally agreed on their excellence, but some considered them to be 'too expensive'. In 1977, the 280E retailed at £8,495, and this did not include a radio, sunroof or electric windows. A Jaguar XJ6 was roughly £2,000 less, and appeared, therefore, to represent better value for money, especially in view of the Jaguar's ride quality and performance.

Much of the Mercedes' high purchase price was due to its construction, which few took into account when offering criticism in motoring magazines. By strengthening the central passenger cell, including the four doors, and front bulkhead, the bodyshell had been made significantly safer. At the same time,

the front and rear 'crumple' zones were modified to de-form more readily upon impact. Similarly, the steering column was constructed to move laterally as well as forwards in the event of heavy impact.

All of these improvements were under the skin, and would only come to light in unhappy circumstances, but they at least went part of the way towards explaining the cost of a Mercedes.

From the Chair

Unlike the contemporary British and Italian machines of the automotive 'upper crust' there was nothing especially grand about the W123's interior. As *Motor Sport* put it, there was 'just the usual Mercedes amalgam of functional completeness without frills, almost austere in appearance in comparison with Jaguar's leather and walnut luxury'. The writer added that this was 'no criticism of either make; it would be a boring world if different tastes could not be catered for.'

The neat facia was in soft plastics – wood veneer featured on the range-topping model – and the upholstery a mixture of cloth and hardwearing vinyl that was made to last a very long time. The seats were typically firm, supportive and most comfortable and shaped to cater for all sizes and physical formats; some models had head restraints fitted for both front and rear passengers.

A model of clarity, the black-faced Vdo instruments, with orange needles, were limited to three – a central speedometer, combination gauge (left) and a clock (right). Mercedes considered a tachometer to be superfluous; for anyone wanting to accelerate to maximum revs through the gears, gear-change marks were indicated on the speedometer. This was entirely logical, but a tachometer would have been nice just the same.

As another safety consideration, switchgear was kept to a minimum. For example, the

The interior was imaginatively styled, the revised seats were more supportive, and there was improved crash protection for passengers. It was a pleasant vehicle in which to travel, but the only aspect that the W123 lacked was the sporting touch, which contemporary BMWs had in abundance.

combination switch on the right of the steering column controlled the windscreen washers and wipers, indicators, headlamp dipper and flasher. Other multi-function switches served to simplify driving, thereby making it safer.

On the subject of the heater controls it is worth recording the thoughts of *Motor Sport*'s Clive Richardson:

In my job I drive so many cars that adaptability isn't much of a problem, save for one thing: heater

The 230E was the first Mercedes production car with a 4-cylinder fuel-injected engine.

controls. I'm sure there must be a running competition between the engineers responsible for heaters as to who can devise the most confusing and inefficient arrangement. Trying to sort out the new 'automatic' system on a Porsche Carrera 3-litre a few weeks ago made by brain ache. Mercedes obviously sympathise, for while their heating is complicated by individual temperature control for either side of the car, the controls couldn't be more clear and logical.

As usual, the steering wheel was large in diameter, at 16in (400mm), padded at its centre, and with an attractive four-spoke design. Although

the column was not adjustable, no one could complain about not being able to find a comfortable driving position.

As on previous models, left-hand drives had a foot-operated parking brake, whereas right-hookers had a lever on the right of the dashboard. Floor-mounted gear levers had been standardized, but automatics could be fitted with a column change according to customer preference.

Ignoring conflicting and often wholly polarized views about the simplicity, or austerity, of the interior, there was little doubting the pleasure to be derived from driving or riding in one of these cars. Like so many Mercs, the W123 had a construction that reduced the stress that can be induced by modern motoring conditions to an absolute minimum.

Quiet, insulated and refined, this was a first-class machine in the upper-middle sector of the market, contrary to the widely held belief that part of the purchase price could be accounted for by the prestige to be gained from owning the most famous motoring badge on the planet.

Four Pots or Six

Working along the lines of 'if it ain't broke, don't fix it', the 4-cylinder engines in the 200 and 230 W123 remained largely unchanged from the outgoing W115 models. With the 1988cc unit in the 200 producing 94bhp at 4,800rpm and the 2307cc engine in the 230 pushing out a maximum of 109bhp

Both 4- and 6-cylinder cars initially used engines already in production. Levels of refinement were so high that, from the driver's seat, there were many similarities with the expensive S-Class.

at 4,800rpm, both engines produced just 1bhp less than the same units fitted to their predecessors. This slight decrease in power, brought about by the need to reduce fuel consumption, made little difference to the performance of either model, the 200, for example, accelerating reasonably smartly from 0–60mph in 15 seconds, and capable of completing the standing quarter-mile in around 20 seconds.

The 230, by comparison, was capable of the 60mph dash from standstill in 13 seconds and the quarter-mile run in 17.8 seconds, remarkable figures for such solidly engineered cars. Both models were available with unmodified four-speed manual, or three-speed automatic transmission.

The engines fitted to these early cars were good ol' sloggers. Reliable, virtually 'bullet-proof' and dependable, they would go on almost for ever if maintained properly, but were clearly not as smooth or quiet in oper-

ation as their BMW counterparts. By the late 1970s it had become clear that they also lacked power by comparison with rivals. Although in a different class, Volkswagen's Golf GTi – the first and definitive 'hot-hatch' – and its meteoric success fuelled a search among manufacturers for greater performance. With its fuel-injected 1.6-litre engine, the Golf was capable of 112mph (180km/h), and 0–60mph in around 8 seconds. It created something of a benchmark, and its neatly packaged format was much copied. Daimler-Benz was not at this stage at all interested in competing in the 'hot-hatch' market – the A class of the late 1990s would, of course, alter this – but there is little doubt that the Golf exerted an influence on European manufacturers, in terms of power-to-weight ratios.

original engines, normal driving conditions would result in overall fuel mileage of roughly 22mpg (13l/100km); this was improved to 26mpg (11l/100km) with the revised units.

The single-carburettor 1997cc engine in the 200 produced 109bhp (Saab's 2-litre 900 produced 100bhp), and there was a useful 136bhp from the 2299cc, which, by virtue of Bosch fuel injection, had changed the model designation of the 2.3-litre car to 230E (E for *Einspritzung*, or 'injection'). The engineers, ever mindful of the inherent 'lumpiness' of large-capacity 4-cylinder engines, included counterweights on the five-bearing crankshafts. The purpose of this technique was to keep vibration down to a minimum, and it was also used by Porsche on the 2.5-litre 4-cylinder 944. However, there is no doubt that

---

230E (W123) 1972–85

Specification as for 200 except for the following:

Engine

Cylinders	4
Bore × stroke	95mm × 80.25mm
Capacity	2299cc
Compression ratio	9:1
Fuel system	Bosch K-Jetronic mechanical fuel injection
Max power	136bhp at 5,100rpm
Max torque	149lb ft at 3,500rpm

---

250 (W123) 1978–85

Specification as for 200 except for the following:

Engine

Cylinders	6
Bore × stroke	86mm × 72.45mm
Capacity	2525cc
Compression ratio	8.7:1, 9:1 from September 1979
Carburettor	Solex 4A1
Max power	129bhp at 5,500rpm
Max torque	137lb ft 3,500rpm

In 1979, Daimler-Benz debuted more efficient and powerful replacement engines for the 200 and 230. The basic design of the single-overhead camshaft format remained unchanged, but the new units were lighter, smaller and had much improved fuel consumption due to the adoption of hemispherical combustion chambers. With the

a 6-cylinder engine in the style of BMW would have been a superior solution.

The weight of the engines was reduced, and the four-speed manual gearboxes also had casings made of light alloy, Prof Porsche's preferred material for the VW Beetle's 'box back in the 1930s. A five-speed gearbox was offered as an option from 1982, the top ratio

280 (W123) 1975–81

Specification as for 200 except as follows:

Engine

Cylinders	6
Bore × stroke	86mm × 78.8mm
Capacity	2746cc
Timing	Twin-overhead camshafts
Compression ratio	8.7:1
Max power	156bhp at 5,500rpm
Max torque	159lb ft at 4,000rpm

being in the nature of an overdrive for the purpose of economy cruising. Both four- and five-speed transmissions quickly gained a reputation for robustness, and were reasonably smooth in operation, although some journalists criticized the 'notchiness' of slotting the lever into second gear. This characteristic was carried over to the 190 Series cars of the 1980s and beyond.

Designated 250, 280 and 280E, the 6-cylinder cars competed head-on with BMW's 5 Series, the Mercedes serial numbers also defining engine capacity. Both the carburettor 2746cc twin-camshaft and fuel-injection engines, developing 156bhp and 177bhp respectively, were old favourites, while the 2525cc unit in the 250 was new. Developing 129bhp at 5,500rpm, it demanded fuel injection but, with a single Solex carburettor, it was not as smooth as it might have been. Gearboxes were identical to those used in the 4-cylinder cars.

The pick of these was the 280E, even though it was not quite as powerful as its earlier incarnation. The change from Bosch electronic fuel injection to the Bosch K-Jetronic mechanical system, along with the adoption of the air-flow metering device, also fitted to the 280SE, brought power output down from 185bhp to 177bhp.

Torque was also down – from 176lb ft to 172lb ft – but by an insignificant amount. In Britain, this model was only available with automatic transmission.

Of the performance, *Motor Sport* commented as follows:

The 280E's straight-six engine is not capable of producing the astonishing performance of some of the V8 Mercedes, but it does have fine attributes of its own, including a smoothness of feel and sound which is alien to a V8 configuration. As the quoted power figures suggest (maximum bhp at 6,000rpm and torque at 4,500rpm), it loves to rev and the four-speed automatic allows it to do so…

Though cushioned by a torque converter, the engine's crisp response through the range is quite delightful; I could imagine it attached to a five-speed gearbox in a small, light sports car (the 280SL, not sold over here, is neither small nor light). Two-up, the 280E weighs over 1.5 tons so the maker's claimed and believable figures of 0–62mph in 10.8 seconds and 121mph [193.5km/h] maximum are highly creditable.

In 1979, the 250 was modified to give 140bhp, courtesy of a new exhaust system and reprofiled camshaft, and just a couple of years later, the carburetted 280 was dropped from the range. The latter held few advan-

280E (W123) 1975–85

Specification as for 200 except as follows:

Engine

Compression ratio	9:1
Fuel system	Bosch K-Jetronic mechanical fuel injection
Max power	177bhp at 6,000rpm
Max torque	164lb ft at 4,500rpm

tages over the 250, and none over the fuel-injected 280E, other than the fact that it was slightly cheaper.

Diesel Sells

Initially, four diesel-engined models were launched in 1976. Both the 55bhp 1988cc 200D and 64bhp 2197cc 220D were economical workhorses intended for the taxi trade. Both were fairly gutless, but no one made a better diesel than Mercedes at this time, and the cars were virtually beyond criticism in their sector. Anyone seeking performance simply did not buy a diesel Mercedes. The 2404cc 240D gave much better performance, and felt a little livelier up through the gears, but a maximum 65bhp made 85mph (136km/h) on an *autobahn* a bit of a challenge, particularly with a load of passengers and luggage.

The revised 2998cc engine in the 300D would nudge 100mph (160km/h), but this version was not especially cheap to buy. Its in-line 5-cylinder configuration was novel, and provided plenty of scope for debate in motoring circles. Later, Audi admirably demonstrated the potential of the 5-cylinder layout with the Quattro, and Formula One designers would eventually show that a V10 had advantages over a V8 and a V12.

In the last couple of decades of the twentieth century, diesel engines in any configuration have been seen to produce unpleasant, smelly fumes, whether burned or not. They must surely be consigned one day to the dustbin of history, but there was no denying the fuel consumption advantages of these oil burners.

In 1979, modifications to the 200D and 240D, which increased their maximum bhp ratings to 60bhp and 74bhp respectively, saw the demise of the 2.2-litre car. At the same time, the 300D's power was increased to 88bhp, but this was still short of what customers, particularly in North America, really wanted. Despite the imposition of a 55mph (88km/h) speed limit across much of the USA, Americans wanted performance and Daimler-Benz duly obliged, in 1982, with a turbocharged version of the 3-litre engine. Developing 125bhp, the 300TD was a useful, practical vehicle for Americans – it was not available in other markets – and its sales quickly outstripped those of the other models.

Springs, Rotors and Balls

Suspension was independent all round, with double wishbones, coil springs, telescopic dampers and an anti-roll bar at the front, and semi-trailing arms, telescopics, coil springs and an anti-roll bar at the rear. With increased track, the roadholding and handling were to Mercedes' usual high standards. With a nicely balanced chassis with initial understeering characteristics, the car was a typically well-honed rear driver.

Motor Sport was particularly complimentary about this aspect of the car:

> There is little roll and the car feels superbly taut with better response and without the harshness of a BMW. Its cornering powers are splendidly high in both dry and wet conditions, very noticeably better in the wet than the S-Class cars. There is a modest amount of understeer normally, but if pressed hard the tail will start to move, without any abruptness. Response to quick changes of direction at speed is simply excellent, an attribute I was already aware of from a four-up demonstration by M-B Chief Test Driver on the Stuttgart test track last year. Such behaviour could mean life instead of death in an emergency avoidance. Straight-line stability is good.

Ride quality was sacrificed a little for the superb roadholding characteristics – it was typically firm – but, while many cited Jaguar's

XJ6 as the master in this respect, the car from Coventry had a tendency to wallow.

Braking relied on servo-assisted discs all round – 10.94in in diameter at the front and 10.98in at the rear – and there was even a pad-wear indicator light on the dashboard. This is one area of car design that had come on in leaps and bounds, and brakes did not get

much better than the Merc's. With wonderful feel, good bite, no fade and tremendous stopping power, they inspired confidence and added to Daimler-Benz's worldwide reputation as a maker of the safest cars. From 1980, ABS was offered as an extra-cost option. (In the 1950s, it was Daimler-Benz that had trailed well behind Jaguar in the braking department. Equipped with Dunlop discs, Jaguars held a distinct advantage at circuits such as Le Mans, where Mercedes soldiered on with vented drums. The latter even came up with an air-brake system for Le Mans,

The first estate versions of the W123 entered production early in 1978, and were clearly aimed at providing competition for Europe's definitive estates from Volvo.

whereby the rear bodywork could be made to flip up before a corner in order to slow the car down. It worked well, too, but not as well as Jaguar's 'infernal' discs.)

The W123's steering mechanism relied on Daimler-Benz's trusty recirculating ball, with power-assistance as an-extra cost option until 1982, when it became a standard feature. Like so much on this model, it could not be faulted in any way, and still feels modern by today's standards. With just three turns of the high-geared wheel from lock to lock, the steering gave a good sense of balance and control. Journalists of all persuasions considered it to be the best.

All Said and Done

The four-door W123 was a European mid-range saloon of the very highest-quality engineering. Although expensive to buy initially, it proved over a long period of use to be good value for money, with residual values always remaining high. Some failed to warm to what they perceived as bland, or even dull, styling; they chose BMWs or Alfas instead. True, some of the post-war Alfa Romeos were visually dramatic and offered out-and-out performance, but the Fiat-owned company always had a reputation for producing cars that rusted badly.

Mercedes appealed to more conservative tastes. Mercedes devotees, who dramatically increased in number during the 1970s, took to the W123 in droves, despite the increasing popularity of fine cars from Munich. For those who wanted something a little more exclusive, without going to the expense of an S-Class, the graceful coupé version was just about perfect.

Cutbacks

The two-door coupé version of the W123, an elegant shortened version of the saloon, with pillarless doors and lowered roofline, arrived in dealers' showrooms halfway through 1977. The various models were launched piecemeal in different markets. Model designation was similar to the saloon range, comprising 230C, 230CE, 280C, 280CE, 300CD and 300CD Turbodiesel. For what was intended as a Mercedes with a very 'upmarket' image, the 4-cylinder petrol-engined vehicles and diesels did not quite fit the bill, but, as luxury cars that were also curiously economical to run, they enabled Daimler-Benz to broaden its customer base even further afield. Japanese manufacturers in particular were beginning to make big inroads into European markets, with all sorts of machines that were ostensibly value for money, and other car makers were sensibly casting their nets wider.

In the North American market, the coupés, like their saloon counterparts, were fitted with gawky, extended bumpers. The Americans were treated only to the range-topping 280CE and 300CD, and the vast majority were sold with automatic transmission. In terms of performance they were virtually indistinguishable from the saloons; after all, they shared the same mechanical components. Volvo similarly built a 2-door coupé, the 262C, in some respects the Merc's nearest competitor. However, the sleek Swedish car had a limited production life and was not especially successful.

With a wheelbase 4in (100mm) shorter, the coupés had the disadvantage of less rear legroom, but the advantage of handsome looks. It was not intended in any way to appeal to the sporting fraternity, but the coupé was a swish tourer, especially in 2.8-litre form, which, although far from grand in the S-Class sense of the word, was certainly approaching the traditional GT class.

Visually acceptable with the standard steel wheels and hubcaps, but greatly improved in appearance with the addition of the smart, multi-spoke optional alloys, body colour was very important with these cars. In traditional

As a load carrier the Mercedes was just about on a par with the Volvo; both were made to the same high standards, but the Stuttgart machine was instantly more prestigious.

black, silver or white, they have an aura of Germanic tranquillity and efficiency, while certain other colours render the car largely undistinguished.

Although the last of these cars were built in 1982, many survive today in superb condition. Many were owned by true enthusiasts, who maintained them as recommended and intended by Daimler-Benz. Correctly regarded as classics among classics, they are highly collectable and continue to command premium prices.

Regrettably, there was never an official convertible version of this car; the additional weight of essential body-strengthening panels, subsequently high purchase price and limited market would have given Daimler-Benz's financial advisers more than a headache.

Backscratcher

The W123 estate car was added to the range in 1978. Unlike so many station wagons based on three-box saloons, the styling of the Mercedes was well balanced – a solid piece of well integrated design. For many years, Volvo's immortal load-lugger was considered by many as the definitive European estate car. Its many qualities – reliability, durability and solid

Swedish build quality – won the attentions of thousands throughout the world. It was a load-swallowing workhorse that seemingly went on for ever, and a bit more. In more recent years, it has even been accorded classic status, while its saloon counterpart is virtually (though not wholly) ignored.

Peugeot's 505 and Citroen's CX estates were also natural competitors in this market, at a time when the so-called multi-purpose vehicle (MPV) had yet to arrive. The models in the Mercedes line-up included the 200T, 230T, 230TE, 240TD, 250TD, 280TE, 300TD and 300TD Turbodiesel. The 'T' appellation stood for *Touristik*; clearly, there was a similar motivation at BMW, which named its estates 'Tourings'. The Munich

company introduced its first estate – the '02 Touring – in the early 1970s. More in the nature of a sporting hatchback, it was the first of a new breed of 'lifestyle' cars, which would become especially popular in the 1990s. The Mercedes estate, though, was not in this league. It was more in the Volvo mould – a smart, no-nonsense purveyor of middle-class families with lots of baggage.

The Mercedes had an extended roof over the hind quarters, a top-hinged rear door,

The cars were so well made that, many years after production was halted, thousands are still in daily use all over the world. One of Daimler-Benz's most profitable cars, the W123 is correctly accorded classic status today.

149

additional side windows and, to keep everything on the road when fully laden, pneumatic self-levelling rear suspension was standard. Smart roof rails, which allowed further baggage to be carried aloft, set a trend that other manufacturers would copy. Like the Volvo, the Mercedes could be fitted with an additional seat in the rear load area. Intended for children, it faced the rear and could be folded flat into the floor compartment.

Although production of the estate ended in 1985, after an extremely successful run, many of these cars are still in daily use, particularly in Britain, where they continue to

With stiffer rear suspension, the estate was arguably a better-handling car than its saloon counterpart. Diesel versions served taxi drivers well, as diesel Mercs had for decades.

change hands for 'old-banger' money. And television news reports from almost anywhere in the Middle East or Africa usually show a W123 driving by in the background!

And What of It?

The 1970s certainly threw up unprecented challenges for the engineers working for car companies. Attempts to stay ahead of, or simply comply with, the differing requirements of so many world legislatures involved having to make compromises in design. Safety had been the burning issue of the 1960s. The reduction of fuel consumption and exhaust emissions were the new concerns for the 1970s.

Little more than half a century after inventing the motor car, and having been

responsible for the development of many crucial safety features, Daimler-Benz was being told by politicians and accountants how cars should be built. They, along with everyone else, were forced dutifully to comply.

The W123 saloons, like the Saab 900, BMW 5 Series and others of similar ilk, were all the result of 'new-age' thinking in the motor industry. Safe, sure-footed, spacious, well-constructed and long-lived, they have all borne the ultimate test and rigours of time.

Writing in *Motor Sport*, Clive Richardson concluded his report on the W123 with the following:

> The Mercedes-Benz 280E is yet another example of superb and honest Mercedes engineering precision and in its own way, bearing in mind its size and engine capacity, I think it is possibly the best volume production Mercedes yet.

Astronomical sales figures bear out Richardson's conclusion. The W123 was certainly a best-seller, but it was also important in establishing the Mercedes name among people for whom motor cars were simply a smelly and noisy means of transport. These people, the antithesis of the enthusiast who consumes as much information as possible on all kinds of car, are a marketing man's nightmare. Mercedes-Benz, and others, spend millions every year bringing their products to the attention of the public. Advertising campaigns, expensive motor-racing activities and the rest were, and remain, part and parcel of moving metal out of showrooms, but the message continues to fail to filter through to some.

The W123 did much to redress the imbalance between those in the know and those who could not care less. It brought Mercedes motoring to a wider audience because of the kind of car that it was. To some, the three-pointed star on its radiator shell was little more than a symbol of social status, an outward display of affluence, or even of arrogance, because of its nationality. To others, BMW drivers in particular, it was just a 'bloody taxi'.

From the beginning of the 1980s onwards, the way in which cars were marketed became as important as the work of the engineers and designers responsible for their existence. BMW's clever advertising campaigns and deliberate policy of spending lavishly on dealer outlets increased competitiveness among all the manufacturers. No matter how good it was, any car had to have an image that fitted the corporate identity. A Mercedes racing car, whether saloon, F1 single-seater or sports-racing machine, had, in some way, to resemble the company's products that ordinary people could buy and drive.

During the 1990s, German car makers in particular spearheaded campaigns of image 'cultivation' even further. The showrooms of Daimler-Benz, Porsche, BMW, Volkswagen and Audi were as much the product of clever designers as the cars they housed. Smartly dressed salespeople offered courtesy and coffee to anyone who looked like a customer with money to spend. There were magazines to read and trinkets to buy, from model cars and watches to clothing and keyrings, and even teddy bears. Everything was emblazoned with the manufacturer's logo; doubtless young Hugo Hakkinen has a Mercedes-Benz teddy bear, after his father's efforts at the wheel of the McLaren-Mercedes.

Clearly, some of the cars made *after* the 1960s and 70s are classics. By the same token, not *all* the cars of this era are true classics – far from it. The point is that they all come under the mighty Daimler-Benz umbrella, which continues to move from strength to strength, despite the many obstacles that occur on an almost daily basis. One day, a book covering the period between 1980 and 2000 will surely be written, and Mercedes will have moved on to produce hydrogen-powered vehicles that run on 'auto-pilot'. Computer software will have improved safety, and brought leisure facilities to the cars' occupants. The Mercedes will automatically sense the proximity of a car in front, and will apply the brakes without input from the driver.

Much of this kind of equipment has already been tested and it all seems to work rather well. But for old codgers of my generation, a car should have twin carburettors that need tuning from time to time, contact-breaker points that close up and stop the engine every 6,000 miles, and handling that allows for the tail to be flicked out of line under power. Such features of older classic cars have to a great extent already been dialled out of modern cars, mostly in the name of safety. We can only hope that the good people working in magical places such Sindelfingen will never see fit to make a car that is so efficient that it is entirely without the character that made so many of its predecessors truly great.

8   Mercedes on Track

Throughout many iconic periods since the French invented motor racing in the early part of the twentieth century, Daimler-Benz has demonstrated its commitment to competing at the highest level. Like the other great factory teams, the Stuttgart people went motor racing in the hope of demonstrating the superiority of their engineering on the world's racing circuits   and because it was fun.

Those lucky enough to have witnessed the battles between established manufacturers at events such as the Targa Florio, Mille Miglia, Le Mans and Indianapolis, particularly between the wars, have memories of an exciting activity at its best. The regulations, political barracking and 'prima donna' nonsense that characterize so much of modern motor sport simply did not exist at this time. There were, of course, the usual business pressures, just as there are from sponsors today, but they were of a different kind.

Motor sport pushes human emotion and ability to their limits in its quest to expand its boundaries ever further. The inevitable results – accidents and the occasional tragedy – have often brought about a knee-jerk response from the authorities. For example, when Brazilian legend Ayrton Senna died at the wheel of a Grand Prix car, doing what he knew best and loved most, the authorities in Italy began proceedings to prosecute senior members of the Williams Grand Prix team. It was a piece of pure theatre from the Italians, and the fact that they did not succeed proves the point that they should have known better.

There have been many other occasions when over-reaction has resulted in motor-racing devotees being handed a raw deal. The two greatest road races – the Mille Miglia and Targa Florio – were abandoned completely on the grounds that running fast cars on public roads had become too dangerous.

That Accident

In 1955 the board of Daimler-Benz was faced with a terrible choice. One of its team of 300SLR sports-racing cars, driven by Pierre Levegh, had been catapulted at high speed into the grandstand opposite the pits during the Le Mans 24 Hours. In avoiding Mike Hawthorn's slowing Jaguar, Lance Macklin's Austin-Healey swerved to the left; Levegh, who was fast approaching Macklin, could not slow down and had nowhere else to go. The Mercedes mounted the tail of the Healey and was launched into the crowd, exploding in a ball of flame, and firing shrapnel into spectators. More than 80 people, including Levegh, died in motor racing's worst tragedy.

Hawthorn, who blamed himself for the crash, was understandably inconsolable. He was not to blame. This was a motor-racing accident, albeit on a grand scale, and accidents will happen in high-risk activities. Although the Automobile Club de l'Ouest allowed the 1955 Le Mans to run to its conclusion – for fear of spreading panic if the race were stopped – Mercedes withdrew its entry out of respect for the dead.

By the mid 1980s, Daimler-Benz had returned to international motor racing. Outright victory at Le Mans in 1989 undoubtedly aided sales of the company's road cars.

The company continued its Grand Prix programme during 1955, competing in the final two rounds at Silverstone and Monza, but closed down its racing department at the end of the season. Mercedes was in no way responsible for the Le Mans catastrophe, but the general view of the board was that the company could no longer afford the risk of being associated with a future tragedy. To motor-racing devotees, the decision made little sense – the withdrawal of Mercedes was a huge loss to motor sport. From then on, Germany's motor-racing honours would be upheld by Ferry Porsche and his friends in Zuffenhausen.

Daimler-Benz's truly great days of the 1930s and 50s were suddenly consigned to history, and both Grand Prix and sports-car racing became an arena almost exclusively for teams from Britain, Italy and France.

A Play on Words

At the beginning of the 1961 Formula One season, contested by exquisitely proportioned rear-engined 1.5-litre cars, Stirling Moss drove a Lotus for private entrant Rob Walker. Without a greedy lawyer in sight, the agreement between the two men for the season ahead was sealed with a handshake. It was all that was needed, and typical of the sport in those days, which are regrettably long gone.

During the first half of the 1960s, Ferrari, BRM and Lotus enjoyed great success in

Grand Prix, while Ferrari and Porsche had it all their own way in the many various sports-car championships. In international rallying, in which Mercedes saloons had enjoyed particular success, winners' trophies and garlands were up for grabs. Such was the gruelling nature of so many of the classic events that success was rarely dependent upon someone having the fastest, or most highly developed, car. Winning a championship was never necessarily the result of spending more money than anyone else. A Mercedes saloon was an expensive car to buy, but this in no way guaranteed it a victory in an event such as, for example, the East African Safari Rally.

In both 1960 and 1961, the International RAC Rally Championship was contested by all manner of machinery, but the eventual victor in both years was Bill Bengry in his bright red Volkswagen Beetle. Bengry's car was run in virtually standard form, except for some spot-lamps, adjustable Koni shock absorbers and larger venturi in the single Solex carburettor. Volkswagen Beetles had also claimed victory on the East African Safari on no fewer than four previous occasions, the final victory for the little car coming in 1962, despite stiff competition from much more powerful cars.

At club level, rallying was usually run at night on public roads, and contested by people in cars that were also used during the week for ordinary transport. To have considered fitting rollcages, sequential gearboxes similar to those fitted to motorcycles (and modern rally cars), special tyres to suit different conditions and the rest would have been greeted by the sporting fraternity with gales of laughter.

At 'clubbie', national or international levels, rally drivers were usually, but not exclusively, amateurs, with a 'proper' job Monday to Friday. Prize money was usually unremarkable and rivalry was friendly. There were disputes, of course, but no one would resort to a court of law to allow a judge should determine the winner. Unfortunately, behaviour would

change in the ensuing years, as more money came into the sport.

In recent years here have been many efforts to recapture some of the atmosphere of old-style rallying. Historic events have flourished in Britain and mainland Europe, and, for the most part, they are good-natured, well-intentioned and exceptionally well supported.

Stuttgart Off-Road

With the benefit of hindsight it is surprising to record the fact that Daimler-Benz supported a rally effort. For so many years, this elitest company had brought glamour to the higher echelons of sport, when it had thrown megabucks at Grand Prix and sports-car programmes. Rallying was considered a rather less sophisticated diversion, but one with great commercial potential. Thousands of ordinary motorists took an interest in rallying – spectators were better able to identify with the cars, after all – and Mercedes, Saab, Ford, Rover, Peugeot, Citroën, and many others sought to make handsome capital.

Mercedes was ready to support a works rally effort by 1955, and Werner Engel, in 300SL Gullwings and 220 saloons, took the European Championship. (Incidentally, it is interesting to reflect that the exotic sports/GT Gullwing provided ideal transport in the rough and tumble of rallying. It was easily the fastest roadgoing machine of the 1950s, and among the strongest, its multi-tube 'spaceframe' chassis proving its worth time and again.)

Alongside Engel's successes in 1955, Belgian driver Olivier Gendebien took a Gullwing to outright victory on the 1955 Liège-Rome-Liège outing. His victory was all the more creditable for having been accomplished without support from the factory. The 300SL was a formidable motor car; capable of a top speed of 155mph (250km/h), with the highest available final-drive ratio. It is still capable of competing on even terms with modern machinery such as BMW's beautiful M3 coupé, even if the expense of doing so might be unbearable. In 1956, Walter Schock drove a Gullwing to victory on the Acropolis Rally, a notoriously rough event, probably giving a few Greek spectators something to think about. Despite its success, the 300SL was not a typical rallying machine, but it certainly set something of a precedent for the Porsche 911 a decade later.

Mercedes' reputation for producing 'survivors' was founded on the Ponton 220 range of the 1950s. The 220, 220S and 220SE were rugged, reliable and solidly constructed, and, although not especially fast, they were better than most at standing up to the punishing terrain of rallies such as the Monte. With all-round independent suspension, 6-cylinder engines and comfortable cabins, drivers and navigators had an easier time of it than many of their competitors.

At the beginning of 1956, a team of 220S saloons was entered for the Monte-Carlo, Walter Shock finishing second behind the equally solid, yet considerably more powerful, Jaguar of veteran campaigner Ronnie Adams. (Adams went on to compete in the 1990 Circuit of Ireland Historic Rally in a VW Beetle at the grand old age of 80.)

Although a number of privateers soldiered on with these cars during the latter half of the 1950s, the factory did not get involved in international rallying until it reappeared with a full works effort for the 1960 season. On the Monte, a team of brand-new 220SE Fintails finished first, second, third and fifth, separated only by the highest British finisher, a Sunbeam Rapier.

Autocar's report on this snow-laden event began as follows:

Challenging the theory, too often demonstrated during the past two years, that the most suitable car for a rally is a small high-performance saloon, three large and comfortable factory-sponsored Mercedes-Benz 220SE saloons have swept the board in

the Monte-Carlo Rally, taking first three places in the general classification, and the team prize. Throughout the event, they were impressively well driven in the icy conditions, and despite many, many miles of high-speed motoring along narrow Alpine roads, they were unscratched at the finish.

It was said that the successful cars, together with drivers and mechanics, had been at Monte-Carlo for three months before the event, practising until the crews knew the all-important Mountain Circuit inside out. This demonstrates, once and for all, that – provided one has sufficient time and money to spare – rallying need not be the lottery that so many people think it is.

That year's Monte was contested by Ford Zephyrs, Sunbeam Alpines, Ford Anglias, Mk 2 Jaguars, Renault-Alpines, ID Citroëns, Austin A40s and even a BMW 700 driven by Princes Metternich and Hohenlohe, but there were also several quietly-stalking horses that went largely unnoticed. On the face of it, BMC's new Mini was a most unlikely rally car, which no one took particularly seriously. In reality, it was an impudent intruder that would prove its worth in the years ahead.

With a unique charm all of its own the Monte was *the* glamorous event on the international calendar. With several starting points in Europe, and concluding in the harbour at Monaco, the event was a test of stamina for all. *Autocar* described part of it in the following way:

A narrow climb out of the town led to the Col du Granier. On the lower slopes the ice was bad, but as the climb steepened and the bends became tighter, conditions were nearly impossible. The whole road was covered with ice, in some places 2 and 3 inches thick. The cars slid and slipped their way up, and delicate throttle control was necessary to avoid excessive wheelspin. To slide on a bend meant one of two things – a sharp halt against a rock or a quick descent over the edge. It was very difficult, and fatal to stop and help push a more luckless competitor. The Moss-Wisdom A40 just made it, and the bigger cars kept going somehow, the Zephyrs and Mercedes 220s being most impressive.

The 220SE's 2.2-litre engine developed 120bhp, every bit of which was necessary for hauling such a large heavyweight around the tight twists of a typical rally venue. The victory by Walter Schock and Rolf Moll, along with the efforts of the other team members, brought Mercedes the team prize on the 1960 Monte. The victory brought criticism of a type that Daimler-Benz had heard many times before, with vitriol being aimed at the German team's thorough planning for the event – clearly a case of sour grapes.

Walter Schock continued the season with huge confidence in his own ability and in the Mercedes, winning outright in Greece and Poland, and scoring high placings in the other events on the European calendar. Championship victory depended upon a high placing in the British RAC Rally; after arch-rival Citroën driver Rene Trautmann crashed out, Schock withdrew his entry. The European Championship was his, but few applauded the manner in which he had achieved it on this occasion.

Mercedes' presence in rallying during the 1960s added greatly to the truly international flavour of the sport. Erik Carlsson's efforts in the same decade in the diminutive two-stroke Saabs have become legendary.

Walter Shock retired from rallying after the 1961 season, and his place was filled by Eugen Böhringer, who ran a successful hotel business near Stuttgart. Böhringer had been incarcerated by the Russians after the war, and drove in the manner of a man who rather enjoyed living.

While Grand Prix racing had attracted very few female drivers, a small number of women excelled in rallying, including Britain's Pat Moss. Ewy Rosqvist and Ursula Wirth from Sweden were enlisted to drive for Mercedes-Benz, in a novel move for such a conservative company. It was a sure sign of the social change that had taken place, and how that change had permeated even the macho world of motor sport. Before the war, works Mercedes Grand Prix aces Rudi Carracciola and Manfred von Brauchitsch had looked down their noses at the 'third' works driver, Hermann Lang, because he had started out in life as a mechanic. They thought themselves far superior to Lang, who outlived the others by many years, and could not only drive a Grand Prix car but also mend one when it broke. How times had changed by the 1960s!

With Finnish co-driver Rauno Aaltonen, who would go on to distinguish himself in all sorts of cars in international rallying, Eugen Böhringer's impact for Mercedes was immediate. His success was all the more remarkable because of the sort of car he was driving; by 1961 rally cars were just starting to become a little more specialized. The Healey 3000 had yet to get properly into its stride, and proved to be devastating when it did, but the big Merc's career was far from over, as Böhringer admirably demonstrated. Third overall in the European Championship was achieved by outright victory on the Polish event and second in the German. A solid steady fourth in Holland, Greece and on the Liège, rounded up with victory in the 1,000 Lakes, where the car was driven by Rauno Aaltonen, rounded off a season that brought Daimler-Benz 'acres' of publicity in the motoring press.

Inspired by his performance in 1961, Böhringer improved the following year. His outright victories on the Acropolis and the Liège and in Poland, and second places in Monte-Carlo and Germany were sufficient for Championship victory. To the surprise of everyone present, Stirling Moss's sister Pat claimed victory at the German event. No one doubted the ability of a woman to win a rally, despite the damage it caused to the ego of some. The really difficult thing to swallow was the fact that she did it in a BMC Mini-Cooper! The locals were somewhat aggrieved to think that a motorized box small enough to fit in the boot of a 220SE could show the establishment, and on home soil, a thing or two about rallying.

During 1962, Ewy Rosqvist and Ursula Wirth took their 220SE to victory on the Argentine Rally, and a similar car in the hands of Rudi Golderer won the Tour of Europe. Of all Mercedes saloons, the 220SE was by far and away the most successful, a small number also being campaigned by wealthy privateers. By the end of this season, British journals were flying Union flags at full height. Some correctly predicted that anyone who wanted to win rallies in future would do well to invest in a Mini-Cooper. In saloon-car racing, the Lotus Cortina was on the brink of supremacy, and Graham Hill had finally given BRM the Grand Prix Championship victory that had eluded Sir Alfred Owen's company for so long. In international sports-car racing, Enzo's 'bloody red cars' were doing rather well, while Porsche was all-conquering in the class for 1.5- and 1.6-litre cars.

Sporting Response

Although the 220SE continued throughout 1963 as a successful car – Ewy Rosqvist and Ursula Wirth won the ladies' prize on the Monte – Daimler-Benz altered focus to the 300SE saloon and the newly launched 230SL 'Pagoda' sporting machine. At around 3,500lb (1590kg), the 300SE was roughly double the weight of a BMW 700 coupé, the diminutive rear-engined car that was enjoying considerable success in German saloon-car racing. The Mercedes, although more robust and reliable than most, was clearly at a disadvantage. Its 3-litre 6-cylinder engine developed a healthy 160bhp, but engine performance of this magnitude was

largely irrelevant in a car that needed to go on a severe diet.

On the 1963 East African Safari Rally the late Bill Bengry, a fine character of the motoring world, followed a Fintail for a while in his works Rover 3-litre. He had time to study how inefficient the Mercedes' independent rear suspension was over the rough, dusty roads of Kenya. 'The bloody thing kept hitting its arse on the road all the time,' he recalled. 'The Rover, with its old-fashioned back axle, never gave us a problem once.' (As an aside, Bengry parted company with Rover after a disagreement over the tool kit provided by Rover for works drivers and their navigators. He felt it was completely inadequate, but Rover's competition management could not agree. Bengry continued his successful rally career in a string of other cars, and Rover's fate is only too well known.)

Despite misgivings from some quarters that the careers of the 220SE and 300SE were on the brink, Daimler-Benz enjoyed yet another highly successful season. Eugen Böhringer spearheaded the company's attack once again, and walked away with a win in Argentina, and on the Acropolis, on both occasions in a 300SE. Not known for doing things in half measures, the company debuted the brand-new 230SL on the Spa-Sofia-Liège, one of the toughest rallies on the annual calendar. Just a few weeks earlier, Rudi Uhlenhaut had demonstrated a standard 230SL to the press at a French racing circuit. Despite a comparatively paltry 150bhp from its 2.3-litre 6-cylinder engine, Uhlenhaut posted similar lap times, on the very same day, to works Ferrari driver Mike Parkes in a 3-litre 250GT Ferrari.

Using a 230SL fitted with a special, experimental 2.5-litre engine, Böhringer and his navigator Klaus Kaiser won the 1963 Liège by a full quarter-hour from Erik Carlsson in the little two-stroke Saab 96. Like its saloon counterpart, the 230SL was an extremely strong, reliable rally car, with splendid handling and great comfort for driver and navigator. Comfort was of great benefit on long rallies, where fatigue could mean the difference between victory and defeat. The mind boggles to think how Paddy Hopkirk, for example, managed to pilot the Mini-Cooper to victory on the 1964 Monte-Carlo Rally. Works Minis may have been great rally cars, but they left everything to be desired in terms of comfort.

The 1964 season was a little less successful for the people in Stuttgart. The 220SE had become long in the tooth, and the 230SL was seemingly outpaced. On the Liège, for example, Böhringer's 230SL finished third, approximately half an hour behind the winning Austin-Healey 3000. British cars – most notably the Mini and the big Healey – were on the attack. It would be another four years before German cars would dominate the international rallying scene again, but it would be Porsche, and not Mercedes, who would show the rest the way home.

Power output of the 300SE's in-line six was increased to as much as 190bhp, and a five-speed gearbox was fitted for the 1964 season, but Böhringer's victory in the Argentine was the only significant success of the season. The Belgian pairing of Crevits and Gosselin in a 300SE won the Spa-Francorchamps 24-hour race, an event demanding the kind of reliability that German engineering traditionally provided in abundance.

At the end of 1964, the factory pulled the plug on its rallying activities, having proved everything that it needed to about its products. No one had been left in any doubt about the strength of a Mercedes-Benz, although there would be future efforts by both privateers and the factory just to remind onlookers that the three-pointed star had not gone away for good.

In the second half of the 1960s, the rallying world would witness the rise of Ford, Porsche, Lancia and BMC, while Saab continued to have an impact. In particular, the Ford Escort,

with its excellent power-to-weight ratio, and fine, agile handling, would almost redefine the concept of a successful rally car. By the mid-1970s it had become arguably the most successful car in the history of the sport, clocking up victory after victory in the hands of drivers such as Ari Vatanen and the late Roger Clark.

Daimler-Benz indulged in an eccentric diversion in late 1968, when Erich Waxenberger, who had been responsible for the development of the 300SEL 6.3, took two of the gargantuan cars to Macao for the annual 6-hour race. A 6.3 was the most unlikely of racing cars, and there must have been many onlookers at Macao who felt grateful that they did not have to foot the fuel bill for the two cars, but the effort turned out to be a worthwhile one. Waxenberger's cars finished in first and third place. The concept of the car as a racing machine was far from the image that Daimler-Benz wished to create for this model, but this did not prevent Waxenberger from preparing three cars for the Spa 24 Hours in 1969. With 6.8-litre engines, they were driven by Rauno Aaltonen/Dieter Glemser, Jacky Ickx/Hans Herrmann and Erich Waxenberger/Kurt Ahrens. Despite meticulous preparation and the distinct advantage of employing the services of the world's best-ever racing driver, Belgian genius Jacky Ickx, the cars got nowhere. Running on standard tyres, demanded by race regulations, they deposited large quantities of tread on the fast Belgian circuit, and spent valuable time in the pits having their wheels and tyres changed. It is doubtful whether the outcome would have been much different if special racing tyres had been fitted. These were heavy cars and tyre producers simply could not cater for them.

The project was quietly wrapped up. The episode had been interesting to motor-racing fans, and particularly so for the great enthusiast Erich Waxenberger, but Daimler-Benz did not approve and that was that. Bill Bengry's efforts with a Rolls-Royce Silver Shadow on the 1970 London-to-Mexico Marathon Rally similarly proved that luxury heavyweights do not have an automatic passport to success in competition.

Return of the Light Brigade

For the greater part of the 1970s Mercedes played no part in rallying, circuit racing or any other branch of motor sport, and more or less allowed BMW to creep in, not through the back door, but boldly through the front. However, the factory took great interest in the 1977 London-to-Sydney Marathon, and prepared a number of 280E twin-cams, ostensibly for use by private entrants. Developing a reliable and eminently usable 185bhp, the cars were prepared to Daimler-Benz's daunting standards.

The stamina needed by the crews for this event made the majority of rallies seem like child's play, and the route also took a huge mechanical toll. Englishman Francis Tuthill, who competed in his VW Beetle, equipped his car with a spare engine because, in his view, 'Sitting in the middle of nowhere without a discernible means of propulsion is not a lot of fun.'

This was an expensive event, guaranteed to consume huge quantities of fuel. The fact that it was being run so soon after the 1973 oil crisis demonstrated that the politicians who had orchestrated the whole rumpus had resolved their differences, at least temporarily, and that the motor industry was well into recovery.

After several weeks of slogging across a number of countries, a brace of Mercs rolled triumphantly into Sydney ahead of the pack, the first driven by Andrew Cowan and the second by Tony Fowkes. It was a testament to the manner in which Daimler-Benz built its cars, and to Cowan's remarkable physical and mental strength. The canny Scot had also won the 1968 Sydney Marathon at the wheel of a Hillman Hunter, the 'cooking', production

version of which was one of the most undistinguished 'sheds' ever to emerge from the Rootes Group.

In 1978, the 280E was also used for the South American Marathon, but without success because Daimler-Benz had also fielded a team of 450SLCs, which were, inevitably, much faster. A year later, Andrew Cowan finished in fourth place on the East African Safari, and in 1980 he drove a 280CE – the 2-door coupé version of the 280E – in Argentina, but without success.

Think Tank

The 450SLC was not a saloon car, but it played such an integral role in reviving the company's interest in sport, so it is worth a mention here. In 1978, the company entered a team for the Vuelta a la America del Sur, an 18,000-mile (28,800-km) 'epic' through South America. The event was similar in spirit to the Carrera Panamericana road races in which Mercedes had been so successful during the 1950s.

On the face of it, the four Mercedes entered by the factory were wholly unsuited to the task of rallying. Automatic transmission and a 4.5-litre V8 with 225bhp in a heavyweight GT was quite laughable. But it was Mercedes who laughed loudest. Cosseted in comfort, Andrew Cowan drove home to an easy victory.

With the full 5-litre engine in the 450SLC for 1979, Hannu Mikkola, who would go on to score countless victories for Audi during the 1980s, finished second on the East African Safari, and won outright victory on the Ivory Coast Bandama Rally. The latter saw Mercedes in the first four places, giving the competition department huge confidence for the 1980 season.

However, things did not go exactly to plan, despite a massive effort on the part of the team. Although remarkably strong, reliable and durable, the cars were not quite quick enough. Bjorn Waldegard scored the only victory, on the Ivory Coast Rally. The team's confidence had suffered a blow by the end of the season – fourth overall in the Championship was nothing to be advertised as a typically Germanic success. On top of this, the company's relationship with the German press had been less than happy and the power of the pen proved more effective than the 240bhp produced by the 450SLC's V8.

The team's initiative to compete the following year with the 190E Cosworth was promptly shelved, and Daimler-Benz's affair with international rallying was at an end. It is doubtful that the 'Cozzie' would have been anything other than a technically interesting, visually stimulating also-ran. In 1980, Dr Ferdinand Piëch had made plans to revolutionize the whole concept of the rally car by launching the Audi Quattro, the turbocharged 5-cylinder machine, with permanent four-wheel drive, that would prove all-conquering at least until the mid-1980s.

In 1980 a team of 450SLCs was entered for the East African Safari. According to *Motor Sport*, they were 'impeccably prepared and looked brutally purposeful, but not even the long stints of meticulous computer-recorded testing of last year were able to show up the defects which were the team's undoing during the rally itself. There is no harder test than actual competition and under the rigours of the rally hub failures resulted in loss of wheels and huge chunks of penalty which put the cars out of the running.'

Two Datsun 160Js placed first and second on this event, with Vic Preston's Mercedes finishing third. As *Motor Sport* added, 'The Datsuns were lighter, not so very much slower, more reliable and certainly mechanically simpler than the Mercedes, with the result that the Japanese service stops were invariably brisker than those of the Germans. What is more, the Japanese mechanics were able to make precautionary component changes fairly quickly whereas the Stuttgart people either had no time for this or had not built it into their service plans.'

With the wisdom of hindsight, the original decision to run the 450SLC as a rally car was bold, brave and slightly eccentric. Its demise was timely.

9 Guide to Purchase and Restoration

Many of the classic Mercedes-Benz saloons from the 1960s and 70s personify Teutonic efficiency and presence at their best. None has the cult status of, for example, the Volkswagen Beetle or Type 2 Transporter – indeed, nothing has – but, as symbols of elitism, quality and sheer engineering know-how, there is little to compare.

One knowledgeable editor has defined a classic car as 'the one you always promised yourself when money allowed'. The choice of that one special car is, naturally, subjective and personal. Some get excited about an MGB, Triumph Stag or Jaguar XJ6, while others dream of a Mercedes, BMW, Porsche or Beetle.

Since about the mid-1970s, the classic car movement has grown, thrived, prospered, toppled, contracted, 'bottomed', and evened out. In some cases, many of the vehicles left to rot in scrapyards in the 1970s were salvaged, restored and cherished. There was a time when a Porsche 356, for example, commanded little more than the price of a 'knees-up' in an English pub; the case is very different today.

Mercedes saloons, by their very nature, were often used as workhorses, family hacks or taxis that, after clocking up a huge mileage, would simply reach the end of the line. The examples owned by fanatics, by contrast, were usually kept in tip-top condition, maintained and serviced meticulously, and driven sensibly.

As the value of classic cars rose, particularly during the 1980s, many jumped on the bandwagon, including those who had never previously had the slightest interest in cars. The classic car became a subject for investors, but, in 1989, the market returned more or less to normal, and many owners lost their money. The investors turned to other projects and car enthusiasts were left to their own devices once again.

Buyers' Guide

When considering the purchase of any old car it is important to have some sort of affection for the particular model. Buying an old car in the hope of making a handsome profit is a sure-fire way of losing money. Performed to the required standard, restoration work is very expensive, and the costs will never be recovered if the car is to be sold on. It is always worth remembering, too, that a ground-up restoration of a diesel-engined 200, done properly, will cost almost as much as bringing a 3.5-litre cabriolet back to life.

The days of discovering a low-mileage 600 in a barn, with an asking price of 'a fiver to take it away' are not quite over, but are becoming increasingly rare. The common-sense approach of buying the best car you can afford is, therefore, inevitable. Although produced to the highest attainable standards, the earliest of 1960s Mercedes saloons are now more than forty years old. Whether the car has been abused or not, European weather will have taken its toll on the bodywork of an original example and, as body-work is the most expensive part of restoration, its condition is of paramount importance.

Mercedes saloons are generally better at resisting corrosion than most cars but, when rust appears, it does so in the sills, wheel arches, valances, floorpans, bottoms of the doors, windscreen pillars and suspension mounting points. If a bubble of rust is visible externally, the damage will always be three times greater where it cannot be seen. And the cost of replacing headlamp lenses, bits of seemingly insignificant pieces of trim, rechroming bumpers, replacing upholstery and the rest, should not be under-estimated.

Almost inevitably, the best, and most genuine, cars offered for sale will be in the hands meticulous enthusiasts. Many will be a member of one of the many Mercedes-Benz clubs, and this is the first place to start any search.

Mechanically, everything made by Daimler-Benz was fairly 'regular'. With correct maintenance the majority of cars that came from Sindelfingen in the 1960s will go on more or less for ever. Poorly maintained examples will break, and when the bang does occur, remedial work will be expensive and time-consuming. It is also increasingly difficult to find people who actually know how to repair Mercs in the traditional manner. The good mechanics are well known, have a huge reputation and a waiting list of months, even years. Non-specialists are to be avoided.

With a wide choice of variants – 4-, 6- and 8-cylinders, petrol and diesel – model preference is down to the individual. Diesels have curiosity and historic value, but little in the way of performance. Solex carburettors fitted to the petrol-engined cars can be troublesome, but so can fuel-injection systems when maintenance has been neglected. With cars that are laid up for long periods, the fuel-injection pumps can 'dry out', leading to cracked seals and leaking petrol. Needless to say, the overhaul of a fuel-injection pump, or replacement, can be costly.

For those who are new to the idea of running a larger-engined Mercedes from this period, fuel consumption is likely to come as a shock. Today, even quite powerful cars return really excellent fuel mileage – BMW's 750i V12 5-litre, for example, is perfectly capable of returning 30mpg (9.5l/100km) – but technology was not as advanced 30 years ago. There is also the need to consider buying fuel additives for engines that simply will not run safely on unleaded.

With a handful of doubtful exceptions, classic cars, including Mercs, should not be considered as an investment. All cars, whether driven or not, will deteriorate over time. They cost money to run, maintain, insure and garage and, when these costs are taken into account, any profit from a sale will be negated.

Dream Machines

Anyone wanting to buy a classic Mercedes, or any other marque, as a means of reliving or recapturing a bygone age, needs a hard-nosed sense of reality and a sharp memory. Mercs from the 1960s and 70s were good cars, but their machinery is not modern. Older Mercedes do not stop as well as modern ones, they generally consume more fuel, and some feel downright sluggish by comparison. The point is that older classics are not necessarily suitable for the rough and tumble of today's driving conditions. Although the journalists who write for the classic-car magazines frequently claim that a well-restored, or original 'oldie' can be driven to and from the office every day without fuss, in practice this is not really true.

Most owners who pour time and money into their dream machine tend to be paranoid about potential theft and damage. And there are other disadvantages. Traffic congestion, speed cameras and traffic-calming measures, along with soaring premiums for insurance and increasing fuel costs, have all conspired in recent years to dull any enthusiasm for motoring. In addition, any owner of a great classic car is usually bombarded with questions and comments wherever they go, from those tedious people who consider themselves to be experts.

However, beyond these difficulties, and the stifling atmosphere of club concours, there is a world in which classic cars can be driven and enjoyed. Club track days at a racing circuit are increasingly popular, and most worthwhile, and there is still scope for exploring large tracts of free roads throughout mainland Europe, North America, and elsewhere. Indeed, rising before dawn and driving my old car into the emptiness of mid-Wales before the rest of the world is awake is one of my own favourite pastimes.

Cash in Hand

Mercedes devotees have an advantage over those who favour other marques. There is a huge choice among Daimler-Benz's saloons from the 1960s and 70s, and no shortage of available cars. It can sometimes take a lot of effort, time and money to locate the 'correct' car – although the Internet has very much reduced this burden – but that car will be out there somewhere.

Members of the Mercedes clubs normally have the finest cars, and this is usually the best source and first port of call. Advertisements in established and reputable classic car journals are always interesting. A car that has been advertised for months on end, for example, might be significantly reduced in price. On the other hand, it might be a 'shed' that nobody wants.

The trick is to be patient and study the market for a long time before parting with cash; there is plenty of scope for making serious errors. For those who are new to Mercedes, it is essential to get advice about a particular model from an expert. Really keen devotees will derive much from a visit to the factory and superb museum in Stuttgart. Both places are inspiring and serve as a shining example to other manufacturers.

The newest of these Mercedes saloons are now more than twenty years old. Depending upon your budget, mechanical and body condition might be critical. The ideal machine is completely original and lovingly maintained, with few miles and a full service history. Such cars do exist but they do not come on to the market very often; when they do, they correctly command premium prices.

Thanks to the many engineering concerns that specialize in supplying parts, any car can be rebuilt to perfect condition. Components are in plentiful supply and it is possible to find craftsmen with the necessary skills to restore or re-create anything. Conversely, there are many people in this field whose work leaves a great deal to be desired, and you should be aware of their existence.

After locating a car, check it over in every way, and remember that the very best confidence tricksters always come across as friendly and honest. Although originally built to the best standards, a Mercedes-Benz is far from immune to corrosion and mechanical mayhem. Always expect the worst and prepare to be pleasantly surprised. The sills, wheel arches, floorpans, inner wing panels, chassis box sections, roof pillars, boot floor and chromium-plated parts, such as bumpers, are all vulnerable to the ravages of weather and time. If you can see some rust easily, you can be sure that there will also be hidden rust that is three times as serious. Recently waxed paintwork can give a false impression of condition; look beneath the deep shine for any blemishes.

The appearance of the underside of a car gives valuable clues as to its general health and condition. Arm yourself with a powerful torch and crawl underneath. At the very least, the majority of cars will display evidence of oil leaks, superficial rust or worse, particularly in panels to which suspension mounts are attached, and the brake pipes will be encrusted in mud. Oil leaks from the engine and gearbox are rarely fatal, but the rate at which lubricant is seeping needs to be established, usually by a lengthy test drive, and checking levels afterwards. Oil splashed around the chassis will have inhibited corrosion and, on the basis that it is usually cheaper to cure an oil leak than to replace rusty panelling, it could be welcome.

Even after studying the underside of the car, resist the temptation to get carried away and hand over your money. Look for cracks in headlamp lenses, missing or damaged brightwork, dented hubcaps and misaligned doors.

Next, switch on the engine and listen for mechanical health. Mercedes engines of the 1960s – 4- and 6- and 8-cylinder units – have a reputation for being noisy, but this is not necessarily a cause for concern. Intermittent or regular knocks and bangs, along with blue or white smoke from the exhaust pipe, will normally signal that all is not well, although engine rebuilds are generally straightforward. Get a long screwdriver with a large plastic handle; place the tip of the instrument on top of the rockerbox cover, and hold your ear to the handle (men: remove your tie first!), to listen for irregular vibrations and untoward knocking and clattering.

The Solex carburettors can be troublesome, particularly on the early cars. Uneven running at idle, or any other engine speed, and the occasional 'flat-spot' have led owners and mechanics along the well-trodden path of tinkering with adjusting screws, jets

and the rest; this normally results in despair. Even highly qualified mechanics have lost the will to live as a result of trying to fettle a Solex. As my mechanic friend Werner Schatke used to say, 'You can't beat a pair of Solexes, but you can burn them.' Investment in Mr Weber's normally reliable products usually has a restorative effect – for both mechanic and car.

Bosch fuel-injection systems, on the other hand, rarely give trouble, but can be expensive to repair. On a car that is subjected to long periods of disuse, the seals in the fuel-injection pump can dry out and break. For an expert, repairs are easy, but time-consuming and, therefore, expensive. Replacement pumps are available, but their cost can induce in some owners an irrational and unhealthy interest in the products of Mr Ford.

Steering Well

Having meticulously checked the official documents relating to a car, the all-important test drive will reveal the true value of its service history. The condition of the driving seat will give a reasonably accurate picture of a car's true mileage, but before jumping behind the enormous steering wheel, it is advisable to allow the owner to take the first stint at driving.

Drivers who treat the controls and driving itself, and the clutch pedal in particular, as a way of relieving their grudges are likely to shorten the useful life of any car, including a robust Mercedes. The owner of such a car might well be proud of the spotless condition of the ashtray, upholstery, headlining and carpets, but this is of little consolation if the propshaft is 'clonking' and crownwheel and pinion are grinding their way to premature death.

Mercedes gearboxes – manuals and automatics – are as complex as any other, but long-lived and dependable. Early automatics do not change up or down as smoothly as their American counterparts (the Mercs of the 1970s were much improved) but excessively 'jumpy' changes will indicate that a rebuild is at least on the way. Remember, these cars were built a long time ago, and mechanical devices cannot be expected, after many years of use, to operate as well as they once did. And do not expect to find a second-hand gearbox from a local scrapyard.

A well-maintained car should feel taut and firm on the road, with little bodyroll around corners, the brakes should give progressive stopping power and pull the car up straight and true, and the steering ought to be positive and reasonably precise, and instill a feeling of confidence. Worn steering and suspension components will be readily apparent, although an inability to travel arrow-straight, and a feeling of terror at high speed through tight corners, is more likely to be attributable to crossply tyres. Sticklers for originality continue to drive on these antiquated items, while radials are safer, generally cheaper and make a lot more sense.

Money in the Tank

A classic Mercedes saloon as a financial investment is an unlikely proposition, as the cost of keeping, running and maintaining one is likely to negate any increase in value over time. An S-Class from the 1970s has increased in collectability in recent times, and even really good examples change hands for comparatively small sums, but a tired car in need of body repairs, fresh paint and mechanical overhaul will inevitably prove to be expensive. The financial outlay required for a 'ground-up' restoration will far outweigh the car's ultimate value, and the same is true of virtually every other car.

Ownership of a 600, for example, will require enormous financial outlay, irrespective of condition. Their rarity, complexity and standing in the automotive world is undisputed, but they, along with a small number of other models in the saloon range, require the loving attention of an expert who knows them intimately. The services of such a person are not always easy to secure. Most have long waiting lists, charge appropriately high sums for their skills and tend to pick and choose the people for whom they choose to work.

In Britain, some cars, like the early Fintails, are not highly prized and tend to be rare. They do not command hefty sums and are relatively easy to maintain. However, owners need to find an expert mechanic who can service them. There must be few people still working who worked on these cars during the 1960s, and many of the youngsters employed in the workshops of Mercedes dealerships today were not even born when many of the cars were made. Many are unfamiliar with carburettors and contact-breaker points, and will be unable to service such componentry.

Cabriolets and coupés are among the most desirable of all Mercedes, and are inevitably costly to buy. Costs inevitably rise if a cabriolet's soft-top is attacked by vandals.

Generally, the cars produced in the 1970s were of better quality than those of the previous decade. As time went on, Daimler-Benz took steps to improve rust-proofing techniques and, although many models were burdened with power-sapping exhaust-emissions equipment, reliability also improved. In the absence of wanton abuse, the only problems that are likely to occur with the later cars are niggling faults with central locking and electrically operated features. These irritating occurrences can normally be rectified easily, but not when they actually happen.

Central-locking systems, for example, always seem to fail when it is pouring with rain, late at night. Bad Dr Sodt moves in mysterious ways.

Despite the pitfalls that lie in wait for the owner of any old car, classic Mercedes ownership continues to be a rewarding hobby, particularly for those who enjoy washing, polishing and driving a car in first-class condition. For most, however, it is driving that is the real point of all that attention.

A well-preserved original machine or a sparkling restoration effort surely deserves better than to languish under a dust sheet in a garage. Worse is the rusting hulk rotting in an orchard, victim of its owner's good intentions to restore it one day to its former magnificence. Advertisements often read 'Restoration project for sale due to lack of time. Need space.'

Renewal Guide

Beginning with a pile of rusty junk that pops and bangs, and belches choking clouds of blue oil smoke, and ending up with a shiny new runner is possible. However, a ground-up restoration requires dedication, patience and time, irrespective of the amount of money available.

Those who never get around to restoring their dream cars fall into the latter category, and if their houses present a picture of complete chaos, their garages are worse, and completely unsuited to the necessary hours of hard work. Typically, they are full of empty oil cans, broken ladders, cardboard boxes full of damp copies of *Motor Sport* and yards and yards of tangled electrical cable.

Before starting any restoration work, it is essential to clean the garage, discard all useless junk, install lighting, heating and a kettle, thoroughly clean the floor and create a muddle-free workbench. This operation is the first and most important hurdle to overcome, and

will take a long time, but it will pay dividends in the short and long term.

Safety must always come first in any workshop. Batteries must be kept well away from a work area, and petrol tanks must be thoroughly washed and banished from any place in which welding is envisaged. Basic safety equipment must include eye and skin protection, and the manufacturer's instructions and warnings on paint and solvent tins must be heeded.

The next stage is the acquisition of tools and equipment, which is where membership of a Mercedes club could prove invaluable. In some cases it will be possible to borrow equipment such as welding and even hand tools. Club members who have previously tackled a restoration will also be able to dispense invaluable advice. Budgeting for equipment is also important because of the 'hidden' costs. Endless trips for seemingly unimportant items that are actually essential all add to the costs.

Taking a car down to its individual component parts with a view to restoring each to new condition is the admirable intention of many, but few realize how much floor space is taken up by a car in bits. Labelling and photographing removed parts might prove invaluable in returning them to their correct position at a later stage. You do not want a car with a few parts left over, even if it works.

One of the most depressing encounters during any restoration is usually the sheer quantity of body and chassis rust. There are several methods of dealing with it. Shot- or bead-blasting, and sanding and treating with a chemical rust inhibitor can be successful, but for advanced corrosion the only sensible course is to remove it and weld new metal in. Welding is not difficult, but *good* welding takes skill, patience and specialist knowledge. The decision to call in professional help is down to the indi-

vidual. For beginners some tasks, such as accurate panel alignment, are daunting but can be achieved by exercising patience and common sense. Securely clamping two pieces of metal together and running a series of spot welds before joining them with a more permanent weld across an entire seam is often a matter of courage and confidence. Mistakes are easily made, and usually easily rectified, but this can be time-consuming.

The same rules apply to painting; anyone can respray a car but the result will vary according to the skill exercised, and the atmospheric conditions. The choice is down to traditional cellulose or a modern two-pack. The former is easier and safer to use, particularly for home restorations, but the time and sheer hard work it takes to achieve a good finish leads the majority in the direction of two-pack. This modern paint is durable and gives a really first-class finish, but it ought to be left to professional body shops because it contains the deadly gas iso-cyanate; the sprayer must wear full breathing equipment. The slightest intake of the material into the lungs will normally result in serious medical problems and may even be fatal.

There are times during a rebuild when nothing goes according to plan. The endless mess, expense, interruptions, neglected family duty, and 'advice' from 'know-alls' are all destined to deflate the most enthusiastic of egos. The slightest setback may tempt many to give up. It happens to virtually everyone. Those feelings of frustration and fatigue can often be alleviated by closing the garage doors and walking away from the whole project. Enthusiasm should eventually return.

Opposite *DaimlerChrysler's Oldtimer department is able to supply parts for Mercedes cars of all ages, including this vintage Mercedes-Maybach belonging to Roger Collings.*

Renewing window rubbers and seals around sunroofs, and locating broken window winders and replacement headlamp bowls and lenses are just some of the many fiddly jobs that take time. Reupholstering the interior to original high standards can make an engine rebuild look like child's play.

Some tasks will simply be beyond the competence of all but the experienced and skilled, and the same applies to major mechanical overhaul. The majority of car enthusiasts can tackle relatively straightforward jobs, such as renewing brake pads and linings, exhausts, and so on, but engine and transmission rebuilds are best left to experienced mechanics. Detailed workshop manuals are available for the most determined, but they rarely provide the whole picture. Unscrewing nuts securing a cylinder head in the incorrect order, for example, can result in a warped head, and there is plenty of scope for wrecking a crankshaft. Precision engineering requires the attention of someone who is properly trained. The many people who do work for which they are not qualified almost always have to enlist the services of someone else to sort out the resulting mess.

Where engines and gearboxes are concerned, replacement might be preferable to repair. Members of Mercedes clubs tend to accumulate spares by the bucketload, and are useful sources of the major, minor and rare parts. Specialists in the commercial world, including Daimler-Benz, generally serve the market well, but it pays to shop around, as prices do vary. As a rule of thumb, quality is determined by price.

Hydraulically powered gadgets and air-suspension systems are complexities that can cause headaches, especially if the car has been bodged by an amateur with a screwdriver and a pack of gaskets. They can be sorted out but the final bill will make most wonder whether or not it was all worth it.

Mission Accomplished

It is immensely satisfying to finish a restoration and to drive it for the first time. Remember, modern rust-inhibiting applications mean that your dream car is unlikely to disappear in a heap of dust and red oxide merely because of the odd rain shower. Try not to become over-protective of your car; it is better to enjoy an old Mercedes by driving it at every opportunity. When, after many years of use, it begins to look tatty, it can always be restored again. Leaving a car for long periods in the best of heated garages is tempting in some respects, but this will certainly have a detrimental effect on some mechanical components. Clutches and brake systems can seize, electrical components can corrode, and small animals may burrow holes and set up home in the most unlikely nooks and crannies.

For the majority of owners, the biggest headache is how to prevent theft. Without protection, virtually all the Mercs made in the 1960s and 70s can be unlocked and driven away by an experienced thief in less than two minutes. Anti-theft devices, from steering locks to ignition immobilizers and electronic tracker systems, will all have a deterrent effect, and are all worth considering. For those who do not want to modernize their classics with such a device, or cannot on the grounds of cost, the simplest method of disabling the car is to remove the rotor arm from the distributor. This simple action costs nothing and gives peace of mind.

For owners who insist on locking their cars away during the winter months when the roads are salted and gritted, disconnecting the battery and removing both the rotor arm and the road wheels will deter the majority of thieves. Cars with wheels attached make for easier pickings.

In the Real World

Having selected a car that best suits your purposes, and carried out the normal checks that it is not stolen, or still subject to a hire-purchase agreement in someone else's name, the most difficult part of owning a classic Mercedes-Benz lies in discovering the best way of enjoying it.

Some people invest a hefty sum in their all-time 'dream' car, drive it home carefully, then put it away in a garage, covered in bed linen and blankets. They have no intention of taking it out on the road. Surely they are missing the point of the motor car itself? Rain rotting precious sheet metal and stone chippings hitting the bonnet are all part and parcel of driving and, when the shabbiness gets to be too much, restoration is the correct path.

Of course, for many, driving on today's congested roads causes stress, frustration and anger. It is increasingly difficult to feel the freedom offered by a motor car, with traffic jams, speed cameras, temporary traffic lights, badly maintained roads, and high fuel costs. Everything seems to be conspiring to make genuine motoring enthusiasts to think again.

An increasing minority have discovered the delights of unrestricted track days organized by specialist clubs. The opportunity to drive flat out without receiving a speeding fine for either, enjoy a civilized lunch with like-minded souls, and not, should never be missed.

Postscript

The cars produced by Daimler-Benz in the 1960s and 70s were designed and built according to the same philosophy as the modern products of DaimlerChrysler (as the company is now known). As Bruno Sacco, former head of Mercedes-Benz design, once remarked, 'Good design is hard work – five per cent inspiration and 95 per cent perspiration.'

Although the cars of today are less conservatively styled – many are right at the cutting edge – than those of yesteryear, the normal tenets of good taste, class and quality are retained. Even today, the life cycle of a Mercedes is thought to be as much as thirty years. The figure takes into account development of around three to five years, production of eight years and use by several owners during the remaining time.

Computers aid design today but only up to a point. The long hard slog of designing and building a car that is correct for present and future markets is still down to a team of people working with pencils and paper – just as it always has been. In addition to 320 men and women working in Stuttgart for the company, there is an outcrop of fifteen based at Como in Italy.

Under their principal director, Verena Kloos, an international team comprising Germans, Italians, Scandinavians and Spaniards is charged with the interior design of today's vehicles. Further design centres exist in Los Angeles and Tokyo. According to Bruno Sacco's successor, Peter Pfeiffer, who took over at DaimlerChrysler in the spring of 1999, the principal purpose of these studios is 'to make concrete proposals for future Mercedes vehicles and, in so doing, to introduce something of a regional perspective. In addition, their task is to come up with new ideas, to stimulate creativity and innovation. Today, our ideas for design development have their origins in the various trends, handicrafts and ways and life of other countries.'

Currently working on cars destined to be made several years in the future, the Mercedes teams remain very much aware of their responsibilities. Innovation and quality are the norm but, beyond these given bases, there is a continuing policy of avoiding trends of ephemeral fashion and fad. A Mercedes of today must not date quickly and, as ever, must not give the company a poor reputation as a result of premature rusting or a lack of mechanical reliability.

In addition to the important work carried out in the design studios, there are research and development engineers working with large budgets to ensure that the cars of the future are improved in aspects of safety, fuel consumption, performance, and the rest. The cars have changed so much in the past several years, but the basic aims of the company have remained unchanged, and the result is that Daimler-Chrysler continues to make classic cars.

Many car folk claim to have absolutely no interest in modern cars, whether they are classics or not. While admitting that today's cars are superior in almost all respects, the majority say that modern machinery lacks character or style. These people might be right in some cases, but there is little doubt that the car world has changed out of all recognition in the past fifteen years. Some changes have been for the better, but not all. New electronic technology has revolutionized design and the way in which we think about things.

Those who pine for the 'good ol' days' – and not all days in the 'ol' days' were good – can take heart from the following story.

Once upon a time there was a shepherd looking after his sheep on the side of a deserted road. Suddenly, a brand-new Porsche screeches to a halt. The driver, a man dressed in an Armani suit, Cerutti shoes, Ray-Ban sunglasses, TAG-Heuer wristwatch and Pierre Cardin tie gets out, and asks the shepherd, 'If I can tell you how many sheep you have, will you give me one of them?'

The shepherd looks at the young man, then looks at the large flock of grazing sheep and replies, 'OK'. The young man parks his car, connects his laptop to the mobile fax, enters a NASA Webster, scans the ground using his GPS, opens a database and 60 Excel tables filled with logarithms and pivot tables, and prints a 150-page report on his high-tech mini-printer. He turns to the shepherd and says, 'You have exactly 1,587 sheep here.'

The shepherd answers, 'That's correct, you can have your sheep.' The young man takes an animal and puts it in the back of his Porsche. Then the shepherd looks at him and asks, 'If I guess your profession, will you return my animal to me?' The young man answers, 'Yes, why not?'

The shepherd says, 'You're an IT consultant.' Astonished, the young man asks the shepherd, 'Yes, how did you know?'

'Very simple,' replies the shepherd. 'First, you came here without being called. Second, you charged me a fee for telling me something I already knew, and third, you don't understand a thing about my business. Now can I have my dog back?'

The moral of this story will, of course, be well understood by all of those with a passion for old cars and history, and an aversion to the modern world and its mistakes and foibles.

Index